M000312898

A COLLECTION OF
FRIENDS

A Collection of Friends

Jim Rundstrom

Contents

A Collection of Friends/ Jim Rundstrom
ISBN 978-1-0879-2844-9

First Printing, 2020

Foreword

When I was about eight years old, I completed a school assignment describing my father's work and explaining whether I would want a similar job, which of course I did, because it would be fun "to teach and have parties."

My dad's life has certainly been defined by impacting students and socializing with friends, as this funny and warm memoir shows. Full of adventures, life lessons, and touching memories, *A Collection of Friends* showcases his journalistic eye for detail and his heart of gold. True to form, Dad places others at the center, but along the way, we see his character and loyalty, wisdom and wit, as we learn more about what friendship means.

Best paired with a glass of wine and a slice of chocolate cake, or while drinking a greyhound, these stories reflect his love of life and celebrate all who are lucky to call him friend, or Dad.

~ *Tracy Rundstrom Williams*

Friends

Few things have such a huge impact on happiness and the enjoyment, depth and plain fun of life as the friendships we have.

Swedish author Henrik Edberg

Introduction

A COLLECTION OF FRIENDS

In September 2012, at age 70, I was in Fort Worth, Texas, on my way to London with my daughter, Tracy, associate director of the Center for International Studies at TCU. I was her travel companion.

She was headed there to assist students getting settled for a semester of study abroad. When I woke up the morning we were to leave, I told her I was having trouble walking. Since we weren't leaving until later that afternoon, I suggested we run up to the hospital so someone could take a look at me.

I walked into the hospital.

By later that afternoon, I not only couldn't walk out, I couldn't do anything. I had lost all use of one leg.

Instead of London, I spent the next 10 days at Southwest Methodist Hospital. Various tests proved nothing, other than I couldn't walk or even get out of bed. It was first thought I had a stroke, but it turned out, according to several neurologists, that I had a virus in my spine that affected the nerve and my mobility.

During the time I was a patient at the hospital, my nurses made an interesting comment as my cell phone rang constantly. "You certainly have lots of friends," one said.

I'm not sure what the reason is, but I am fortunate to have great friends. *Why* is a good question. Maybe having spent five years as an undergraduate student who enjoyed more time outside the classroom than in it, then having a 40-year career as a college professor and as the university's alumni director at my alma mater put me in contact with a wide cross section of people.

I started my college career in 1959 when I was 17 at what was then Nebraska State Teachers College at Kearney. Four years later the name was changed to Kearney State College. In 1991 it became the University of Nebraska at Kearney (UNK). I was part of all those name changes.

My first major was business. I enrolled in beginning accounting but after missing several classes, I dropped it knowing a person couldn't miss any classes and keep up. I changed my major to physical education since I was on the freshman basketball team. When that didn't work out, journalism became an option. Since I liked sports, writing about them made sense, especially since I had a good English background.

I've shared this story about how I got into journalism. It is more fun than the real story.

My grandfather was a doctor so I decided I might like to go into medicine. I wrote a letter to Dr. Don Fox, chair of the chemistry department at Kearney and a major influence in the lives of most students who went on to become doctors. I explained my background to Dr. Fox in the letter and in a meeting we had.

Dr. Fox said, "Jim, I think journalism would be a good major for you."

"Well, Dr. Fox, is that because you thought my writing in the letter was good?" I asked. "No, he replied, I've seen your high school transcript and you are not smart enough to be a doctor."

Journalism turned out to be a good direction, one that put me into contact with a wide variety of people and created untold friendships.

My friendships that developed from that career and all of those life experiences have enriched my life tremendously, as they do for everyone.

Here are stories about some of these friends.

1

Courtside Manner

Courtside Manner, n: using lessons from sports in everyday life

As I was recovering in the hospital, one of the issues I faced was my plan for physical rehab. My goal was to get back home to Kearney where I had lived for most of my life. Where my doctors were my friends. Where there was family. Where there was a support system. I wanted to go home.

One of the early calls I received was from UNK's basketball coach Tom Kropp. It was the middle of September and coach Kropp was getting ready for the beginning of basketball season practice. In typical Kropp fashion, he simply said, "Jimmy, when you get ready to come home, we will come down to get you. Don't call anyone else. Just let me know when you're ready. I'll get Riess and we'll be there." Riess was in reference to Larry Riessland, another of the truly great friends any person could have.

I've always been amazed at many of the personal qualities of Tom Kropp. He is one of the most decorated Nebraska high school athletes in history. His athletic achievements and his personal qualities are legendary. He was the first Nebraskan named to the national high school hall of fame, he has been inducted into the Nebraska High School Hall of Fame and UNK's Athletic Hall of Fame.

Basketball coaches Kevin Lofton and Tom Kropp

At Aurora High School, in track, he was the undefeated state champion in the shot put and discus. In basketball, as a senior he averaged 33 points and 23 rebounds. In baseball, he pitched a no-hitter in the semi-finals and was the winning pitcher in the championship game. He is considered one of the best football players in Nebraska history.

The high school Shrine Bowl all-star game illustrates that.

One of his accomplishments is when, after that Nebraska Shrine Bowl football game for outstanding high school players, the organizers had to call him aside and tell him that he was named the most valuable player on both offense and defense, but he could only win one of the awards. He chose offensive, since that was what he thought he would play in college. He was that special.

A first team All-American in both football and basketball at UNK, he was drafted out of college by the Washington Bullets of the NBA, the Pittsburgh Steelers of the NFL and the Denver Rockets of the ABA. He played for the Bullets and the Chicago Bulls in the NBA for two years and in Europe for four years before returning to UNK where he began his teaching and coaching career.

An academic All-American as well at UNK, he also earned a master's degree while working as a graduate assistant and later, a doctorate from University of Nebraska Lincoln.

Tom is also a most thoughtful person.

When he is in a room, you would never know anything about his athletic background. All he ever wants to talk about is the other people there. The center of attention is always someone else. There is no one more grounded than Tom Kropp. Plus, he is one of the best and most popular teachers on campus.

And a great story teller.

Hardly a day goes by when I don't run into a student who has taken one of his classes. Their comments are always the same. His stories are great and their messages are even more important.

One of our regular basketball activities was shooting games, a H-O-R-S-E - type game. Coach Kropp organized those shooting games and always invited anyone who wanted to play to join in. He always found a way to include shooters of every ability.

One fall Saturday morning, we were doing shooting games with all the players on the basketball team and a few others including one of Tom's former teammates, Carlos Dillard. Carlos was the only black member of the team when Tom played. Before we started shooting games, Tom divided the teams up, explained the rules to everyone and introduced Carlos to the players. He told them what was a great friend Carlos was.

Kropp said, "Fellas, our friendship is what developed from the two of us playing together and being teammates. When you are done playing basketball, he said, you will remember only one thing, the relationships you developed. Scores will become meaningless. Personal accomplishments won't mean as much. But the friends you made will be with you all of your life."

That point pops up in almost every conversation with former players.

A *Kearney Hub* newspaper story about All-American basketball player Nick Svehla is a perfect example.

The details of the story written by *Hub* sports editor Buck Mahoney are something like this.

If the University of Nebraska at Kearney has a basketball hero, it's Nick Svehla.

The undersized big man delivered a performance of legend, scoring 36 points and grabbing 17 rebounds in the Lopers 2003 win over Metropolitan State, the defending national champion, sending the team to its only Elite Eight appearance. His 3-pointer from the corner with 4 seconds left forced the second overtime in one of the most exciting games in Health and Sports Center history. Everyone there still remembers it as 'The Shot.'

Sure, it's a memory that sticks out in Svehla's mind today, but it's only a blip in the overpowering light of his college experience.

He now understands what Coach Kropp has told his players and everyone else so often – it's the relationships and friendships that are formed during one's athletic career that really matter.

He said he looks back with fond memories of the guys he played with and the relationships they had and still have.

Those were good times. "I had just as much fun outside of playing basketball as I did playing basketball," he said.

When Svehla was inducted into the UNK Athletic Hall of Fame in 2013, a comment was made about 'The Shot,' he made, referring to that 2003 NCAA regional game. After the event was over, his wife asked him what was 'The Shot' they talked about. As significant as it was to everyone else. he hadn't even told his wife. But she knew all about his teammates and his friends from his playing days.

Svehla learned the importance of friendship from coach Kropp, along with many other former players. There was always a lesson in the Kropp stories. His message never changed.

Treat people right was his hallmark.

One of my former journalism students, Craig Larson, shared this story about Kropp when Craig was sports editor of *The Antelope* student newspaper in 1980. He has used the story in his teaching at William Jewell College in Missouri and later in varied positions with the Nebraska Rural Radio Association where he served a CEO from 2011 until retiring in 2020.

In the spring of 1980, Craig was trying to interview Kropp before an alumni basketball game to raise funds for the current Lopers team that was planning an overseas trip that summer.

Just before the game started Loper coach Jerry Hueser called to Tom to tell him they were ready to start. Kropp told Craig that he would talk to him first after the game. Which he did. Since Kropp was home from playing in Europe, a number of other reporters and media people wanted to interview him. Kropp walked off the court and said he would be happy to do so, but he promised the student sports editor he would talk to him first. Craig said that spoke volumes about the kind of person Tom Kropp is.

Loren Killion, Craig Larson, Tom Kropp

Craig was also thrilled to get the attached picture with another All-American basketball player Loren Killion. It's a picture he has always saved especially since he was in the middle. The cutline was priceless, 'Can you spot the two All-Americans in this picture?'

Whether it was the custodian, bus driver, student trainer, they were treated just like the athletic director or the chancellor.

That Saturday morning with Carlos Dillard coach Kropp shared the following story and the value of friendship.

Carlos, remember when I was a senior and we were headed to Omaha to play UNO? Carlos shook his head. Remember we stopped at a truck stop near Ashland for a pre-game meal? Carlos nodded again. Fellas, I had the flu and was really sick. In fact, I seriously thought about not going with the team. But I sucked it up because I was part of that team and that if I got better during the day, I might be able to play that night. I could hardly eat but Carlos never left my side. He wanted to make sure I was okay. Halfway through the pre-game meal, I was really sick and had to get to the bathroom. Carolos followed me. I was standing at the urinal when I got really dizzy, passed out and fell down hitting my head on the floor. It didn't knock me out but did daze me. Carlos was right here to make sure I was okay. Fellas, do you know what kind of friend he is? He got down on his knees, reached over and zipped up my pants. That's the kind of friend he is. He didn't want anyone seeing me like that.

Friends like Carlos are hard to find.

The players were a little reluctant to laugh at coach Kropp's story, but everyone else could see the humor and the message he sent.

Coach Kropp and I were talking one day about recruiting. We were driving to watch a junior college game coached by good friend. It was during the Miami Heat title runs in the NBA. Coming off a 25-6 year, he said that they had good players coming back that year. "Jimmy, we're only a couple of players away from competing for a national championship – Labron James and Dewayne Wade."

I always smiled when he gave the speech to his players about being on time when leaving for the first game. The bus leaves at one o'clock.

Exactly one o'clock. It is the same rule we had with the Chicago Bulls. Coach Ed Badger said, "We leave on time even if we have only five players. Well, unless one of them is Tom Kropp. Then we will wait for a sixth."

All of his stories are as legendary as his athletic accomplishments, his coaching success and his genuine caring for others.

I learned an important lesson in life from coach Kropp simply by going to watch basketball practices. In one of the early-season practices, the players were running lines for conditioning. 'Touch each end line,' coach said. When one of the players came up short at one end, Kropp blew his whistle and said, "Fellas, we don't cut corners. When we run a drill, we run it the right way. Dammit, touch the line at both ends of the court."

Often, when I am exercising by riding my stationary bike, I set a goal for my workout – two miles, three miles, or whatever. Never, thanks to Kropp, do I stop without reaching that goal. There is never any question that I would do it the right way, the Kropp way.

When my wife Lynn died from a stroke in 2012, we had a gathering at the funeral home the night before the funeral. That winter Thursday night, coach Kropp cut practice short and brought every player and coach to the funeral home to pay their respects. They were leaving for Colorado the next morning, but this gesture was important to him.

Things like this defined Tom Kropp.

2

Ries-ses

Ries-ses, n: pieces of a simple life

Larry Riessland came to Texas with Coach Kropp to get me and drive me back to Nebraska where I began therapy. I told them I would be dismissed from the hospital on Friday afternoon after one last test, a spinal tap. They assured me they would be there that morning. I said that I would call them along the way in case there were any changes in my plans. There was silence on the other end of the line. 'What's the problem,' I asked Larry before they left. "Well, neither one of us has a cell phone."

Now remember, this is 2012 and Kropp is the head basketball coach at UNK and Riessland is the director of finance there, a position he held for more than 40 years. If you were to draw a picture of two athletes, you could start with them. They are also terrific individuals.

Larry Riessland is as loyal and genuine as Tom Kropp.

In high school at Pleasanton, a small town north of Kearney, he earned a 'Mr. Touchdown' label where he scored 80 touchdowns in his career. He set a national record nine touchdowns in a single game as a junior, then set a national record with 47 touchdowns in a nine-game season in his senior year. He ran for 2,217 yards as a senior and averaged 19 tackles a game. In basketball, he scored more than 400 points his junior and senior seasons.

Roger Jones, me, UNK Athletic Director Dick Beechner (standing), Larry Riessland, Wayne Samuelson, John Lakey

In college, before his career ended with an injury, he set the UNK punt return record of 89 yards that stood for 28 years.

He is the most self-sufficient person I know. He could live off what he hunts and fishes – elk, deer, turkey, turtle, catfish, walleye, geese, duck, pheasant, and almost anything else that roams his property. A perfect vacation for him is a hunting trip to Wyoming, Colorado or Alaska. Riess lives in the country, along the South Loup River near Pleasanton. I recently told him that if the liquor stores delivered, he would never have to leave his house except to travel with his wife Carol to watch his grandkids play sports. Oh, yeah, and to hunt and fish.

When Tom and Larry arrived at the hospital, I could barely get to a wheelchair. But, here were these two athletic men treating me like I was the most important person in the world. One obstacle was I had a catheter attached to my leg. After we left Fort Worth and headed for Nebraska, we stopped three times that afternoon and evening primarily so my catheter could be emptied. Larry Riessland would bend down, take it off, empty it and replace it. I still have vivid memories of these two guys taking care of me like I was a helpless baby. We made it past Wichita, Kansas, that night. They carried me in to our motel room, made sure I could sleep and checked on me regularly. In the morning, after rolls and coffee, we headed to Kearney.

I wasn't sure what I was going to do when I arrived even though I had thought about it often. In my house, all the bedrooms are upstairs and I certainly wasn't in any condition to go upstairs.

So, they brought a bed down, set it up in the living room and got me settled. On Monday, I met with my doctor in Kearney and he recommended I check into Good Samaritan Hospital for two weeks of inpatient therapy. Those tow guys checked on me every day. I was in great hands with their help.

To use a Tom Kropp line: friends like these are hard to find.

3

Diplomatic Tours

Diplomatic Tours, n: serious and not so serious travels from Kearney around the world

One of my colleagues at the university, Galen Hadley was the dean of the College of Business and later vice chancellor for academic affairs. He has been commissioner of our fantasy football league for years and is commonly referred to as 'Commish.' Galen has a long history of community involvement including being mayor of Kearney. He also served two terms as a Nebraska state senator and two years as Speaker of the Nebraska Legislature. Travel has always been a passion for Galen and his wife Marilyn. My travel memories with them are many.

And fun. And ones that have made good stories.

My wife, Lynn, and I traveled with Galen and Marilyn, to Ireland in 2008. We rented a car for two weeks and drove around the country. I also spent two memorable weeks with them in 2015 visiting Finland, Sweden and Norway.

At one bed and breakfast over afternoon cocktails on our Ireland trip, we began to talk to the owner. My interpretation of the visit is quite different than Galen's more accurate one.

The conversation eventually got to politics when Galen pulled out his card and gave it to her. She looked at it and said, 'You're a senator?' He replied, 'Yes.' Her response, 'Like in Washington, DC? as she got a big smile on her face. 'No, I'm a state senator for Nebraska,' Galen replied.

Actually, it was no big deal in the conversation.

Of course, when we got back home to Kearney I added some new parts. I said the lady was devastated. It was like sticking a pin in a blow-up doll. She just wilted and then wanted to talk about something else. Naturally, I couldn't wait to tell the story to everyone – embellished with my interpretation.

I have always valued the friendship that included me in some of their travel adventures which have taken them to every continent and more than 60 countries.

Galen always likes to have me tell the story about our 2018 trip to Halifax, Canada, and the area around there. As Marilyn and my partner, Ellen, were exploring the depths of the Atlantic Oceans tides, Galen and I waited in the parking lot.

We struck up a conversation with a local guide, who since retiring had volunteered at the park. In what I suppose was a typical question he asked everyone was whether we had come to the area for lobster, a huge tourist attraction. Galen smiled and told him that he, Marilyn and Ellen had, but that I didn't eat fish.

The guide laughed and told the story of growing up in the area. "When I was in elementary school, we had lobster rolls for lunch every day. The rich kids had bologna sandwiches. We would trade two lobster sandwiches for one bologna sandwich." That story gets a head shake from our friends.

Marilyn Hadley, Ellen Morledge, me, Galen Hadley with our
lobster bibs

On a trip to Costa Rico, Galen sent an email picture of a dorado
fish he caught, bragging about how much larger it was than some fish
that his friends had caught. "This is what real fisherman fishes for. Not
a four-inch piranha like JR caught in the Amazon River or a 10-inch
trout he caught on the North Platte River in Wyoming but a huge dorado." It really wasn't that large of a fish. John Horvath, one of our
fantasy football gang from Alaska who has fished for salmon and halibut pointed out to him that "fish that size we use for bait in the North
County."

One of our friends completed his version of the fish story for our
social gatherings. "Immediately after landing the fish, the guide asked
the Commish, "Do you want to mount it?" Galen misunderstood, said
"yes," dropped his drawers and sure enough, he was ready to mount the
fish right there. The guide was too surprised before Commish had his
way with the poor dorado. Galen is a legend of sorts down there now.
The guide no longer uses the word "mount," instead he uses the term,
"take it to a taxidermist."

4

Out-putt

Out-putt, n: the power or energy produced by missed putts; the quantity or amount of putts taken

Nobody could have done many of the things Galen has any better, whether it was in university leadership, local politics or the state legislature.

Or, more importantly, as our fantasy football league commissioner. Through the years our group has met every Thursday during the season to make trades, play pitch and socialize. As the self-proclaimed "World's Greatest Commish," he has always done a great job of keeping track of the league and tossing zingers to everyone in the league – including himself.

He also claims to play golf, but that is debatable.

UNK has an annual athletic department fundraiser called the Blue Gold. Galen was on one of our two six-man teams one summer. Since we get together for cocktails and activities the night before the event, we decided to make a special presentation to him one year.

It went something like this.

Some of you don't know Senator Hadley as well as others of us, so here is a little background on our Speaker of the Legislature, a most important position in Nebraska. In fact, when the governor and the lieutenant governor are out of the state, Hadley is in charge.

I have played golf with hundreds of people through the years but I have never played golf with anyone with the same skill level as the senator.

I have never played golf with anyone with the putting skill of Senator Hadley either. His putting may even rival good friend Jerry Dunlap. Jerry and I were playing in a closely matched contest one year when we came to the 16th hole on his course. Tiburon, in Omaha. Jerry had a 20-foot putt to tie me on the hole. He hit the first putt about 15 feet by, left the second six feet short, pulled the third left by three feet. He finally five putted. How, you ask? I gave him the last one.

One day when we were playing, the good senator hit maybe the best shot I have ever seen him hit. It was on a 155-yard par three, 9th hole at the Kearney Country Club. It came within a foot of going in for an ace. Directly behind the hole. We walked up to the green and I said 'pick it up.'

"Oh, no," he replied, "I'm a stickler for the rules. I'll putt it." Which he did. Blew the first putt by four feet and missed the second one, too. Settled for a give-me bogey.

I have never played with the senator when he didn't begin each round with his famous statement, "I'm a stickler for the rules." He knows the rules. He also has a wonderful and imaginative interpretation of those rules. For example, if a tree is in the way, the ball can be moved since the tree was not properly planted. If playing a water hole, that hole can be skipped to speed up play and balls hit in the water do not have to be retrieved.

It reminds me of a wonderful line by our late friend Augie Nelson. I was playing with Roger Jones in a Minden tournament years ago. A creek runs through the course and Roger hit a ball into the creek in some fashion. Roger promptly pulled out his ball retriever, found the ball and got it back. Augie's comment, "The ball retriever is the only club Roger has ever had to have re-gripped from overuse." It was the first time I had heard that line. The retriever is also Hadley's favorite and most used club.

What's interesting about playing water holes is that Senator Hadley could easily play all the water holes since, as a senator he pointed out, lobbyists provided him with all the golf balls he needed. He doesn't have an old ball. Lost them before they ever had a mark on them.

Finally, I have never played golf with someone who has the same goals as Senator Hadley. As long as I have known him, they have always been the same – make a par every month he plays. It is an admirable goal. It's not very realistic, but certainly admirable.

I'm delighted to see that the senator has a renewed interest in golf. So much so that recently he tried to buy a game. Among his new clubs are two hybrids. He said by using mine the past few years he realized how valuable they were. In fact, as I looked in my bag, my hybrids are missing. And, I have no idea where they went.

With his passion for golf, it seems appropriate that Senator Hadley would have a putter that is symbolic of his lofty position as a legislator and a golfer. This engraved putter says it all - The Original Senator.

I got the putter on-line from eBay. It was one of Austad's original clubs. And, it fit this situation perfectly.

It made a great gift.

5

Smart Guys

Smart Guys, n: friends learning to spell

My long-time friend and golfing partner Steve Lydiatt 'Lyd' and I often walked home after Wednesday night golf since we both lived on the golf course. We played golf together for more than 40 years. When he retired, Steve and his wife Patty, sold their home in Kearney and moved to Monument, Colorado. On that last Wednesday in May 2012, when we walked home together, I cried. I knew that even though we would continue to be great friends, our lives had taken a new twist.

Typically, on those Wednesday nights, we would have a few drinks and dinner along with sharing stories of golf and many other things. Sitting around one night, Steve coined the term SJC or Smart Guys Club for the guys.

When I got home, I promptly told my wife that we had a new group after golf called SJC – Smart Guys Club. She said, 'What's the 'J' stand for?" "Guys," I replied. She just shook her head. Since our country club was small, it didn't take long before SJC became a part of conversation – Are you having SJC Wednesday? How was SJC? Who was at SJC? And things like that. You would think older adults would outgrow that kind of humor but it has stuck.

We weren't great players, but we were good enough to win two Nebraska State Elk's Tournaments with two other guys. The first was in Scottsbluff, about a five-hour drive from Kearney. Lyd, Jon Cole, Jerry Foote and I represented lodge #984. Our friend Wayne Samuelson was exalted ruler. After we won the tournament, we celebrated. Probably too much since we had to drive back to Kearney that evening. We were among the last to leave the bar after we had dismantled the trophy and passed it around for everyone to have a drink from the trophy cup.

There was one other group still there when we said we needed to get on the road with a five-hour drive ahead of us. Those guys smiled. Five hours? We have another five hours from Kearney. They were headed to Falls City, about as far away as you can get from Scottsbluff – more than 500 miles. I'm not saying we had too much to drink but at a Burger King stop in North Platte we drove into the area where the trash bin was located and honked our horn. A young employee came out to tell us that we were not in the drive-thru.

Two years later, we won the tournament in Sidney. This time our foursome was Jon Cole, Jerry Foote, Wayne Gappa and me.

We also finished second twice. One of those times was in Beatrice where we were leading when one of our players, whose handicap was about 30, had only to make a triple bogey on the last hole. He didn't even come close. An out-of-bounds on the right side of the fairway sealed our demise.

We still chuckle about a golfing incident with Jerry Foote, one of our regular Wednesday afternoon group and Elks team member. Jerry lost a ball on the fourth hole, so after looking for it, we suggested it just drop another rather than go back to the tee to hit another. Those were the days when you dropped the ball over your shoulder. That's what Jerry did. Then he turned around to look for it but couldn't find it. "Where did my ball go? Did you see it?' he asked. In searching for his ball, we found it. It got caught in his shirt. Never did hit the ground.

6

Fishing

Fishing, v: searching for river enjoyment on the Platte, Amazon and Kenai

Lyd and another friend, Bruce Elder, offered to take me fly fishing one spring. Both loved to fish and are great fishermen.

Me, I went for the friendship.

Before I could go with them, Lyd made me watch a video on fly-fishing and practice casting in my back yard. I diligently did both and really looked forward to the new experience like a little kid. We camped along the North Platte River near Centennial, Wyoming. It was a popular place that both knew well having fished there often. They prepared me well. I bought my first fishing license. Since I didn't even have a pole, they supplied me with all the equipment I needed, including waders.

We arrived at the campground, set up our tent and headed to the river.

Lyd and Bruce found what look like a nice place for me to try my luck. I waded to the middle of the river and practiced a few casts with them watching. After they had me set up, they went up the river and disappeared around a bend. Ten minutes after they left, a small herd of wild horses galloped up to the edge of the river for a drink. It was an amazing sight and gave me a sense of why fly fishing was such a passion. Here I was, all by myself in a serene setting, a warm sun shining down with the beauty of the mountains and the wilderness. Maybe I could get into this I thought. I tried a few casts, but with no luck and little patience, tired of the exercise quickly.

What I did find was a nice huge rock right in the middle of the river. It was a perfect place for an afternoon nap. When they came back, they found me asleep on the rock. It didn't take them long to realize I lacked the passion of a fisherman. I did catch one trout the next day. It wasn't even with a fly rod. I just snagged him with a regular rod and reel.

Now when they take me fishing, it's only to take pictures of them.

A couple of other fish stories are a bit unusual, too.

The four-inch piranha that Galen Hadley made reference to refers to a trip I made to South America in 2005 with my son-in-law Andy Williams.

Andy Williams, a native Peruvian woman, me on a reed boat
at Lake Titicaca

Andy had connections in Iquitos, Peru, one of our destinations after Lake Titicaca and Machu Pichu.

Andy had made several trips to there and befriended a local guide named Andres. Andres had a campground on the Amazon River for tourists who were interested in a remote visit to the area.

We made the trip to the Amazon camp for a couple of days in the wilderness.

One of the things Andy wanted was for me to catch a piranha.

The first evening we went out on the river in a rustic dugout canoe to try our luck. Getting in the canoe was a bit scary for me since we had to bail water out of it before we left. No luck with fish the first night but we did catch a two-foot caiman.

Catching a caiman and a piranha

After taking a couple of pictures, we put the caiman back the river.

What I remember is the only light we had was the sky above and our forehead spotlights.

Andy told Andres we needed to try again. "We're not leaving here until Jim catches a piranha."

We had no luck the next morning but did that afternoon.

Actually, it was pretty simple.

We used a bamboo-type stick for a pole, several feet of fishing line, a hook and some fresh meat for bait. We stirred the water around the canoe to attract the piranha and dropped the line in the area. With the smell of fresh meat, the piranha swarmed around and I caught a small one.

Back in Iquitos, I bought a mounted piranha just like the one I caught. It was small, the size of my palm. It's the teeth that make it so dangerous.

Several years before the South America story, I caught two salmon in Alaska. Well, I guess you could say I sort of caught them.

Catching salmon with my hands

Many go there to fish, especially for salmon or halibut. I was not one of them.

We were visiting friends Kent and Jane Mattson and John and Kathy Horvath.

One morning, they suggested we walk down to the Kenai River near where the Mattsons lived. Kent's friend had a commercial netting license that allowed him to catch salmon on the river.

After he emptied the nets into the back of his pickup, he would take them to the canary for processing. We got there just in time to see a truckload of salmon.

I reached in, grabbed one for each hand and held them for a picture.

When I got home, I shared the picture with my friend Ed Walker, an avid fisherman. I said, "Ed, you need to get to Alaska. The fishing is incredible. You can catch them with your hands."

7

Bear-ly visible

Bear-ly visible, adv: things very difficult to see

The year after I had my leg episode, Steve and I took a trip to Yellowstone in an effort to clear off a couple of items on my bucket list.

I was five states short of visiting all fifty and two of those were Idaho and Montana. Plus, in all of my travels, I had never seen a bear in the wild. It was one of the things on my bucket list. Lyd said, "We can do both by going to Yellowstone in September."

Perfect, I thought. On the way to Jackson, Steve was driving my car when he said he saw three black bears in the hills in the distance. "There they are far off to the west. See them?" was his simple statement as he pulled off to the side of the road to show me. I couldn't make out any bears. They are there, Steve said.

"Now you can say you've seen a bear."

That was Steve's story

However, there are two versions of the 'bear story.'

My story is more colorful than Steve's which went something like this.

"Runt, Runt, look over there. Three black bears," he said.

Then, he slammed on the car breaks, left skid marks that made the tires on my car bald, flipped a U-turn, just missed getting hit by a semi and pulled over to the side of the road. "See them. See them." He said.

I replied, "Give me my binoculars. They are in the back seat."

I adjusted the binoculars, looked over to the side of the hill and said, "Lyd, those aren't black bears. They are black angus cows."

So, it is a standing joke now when we see a herd of black angus cattle we call them black bears.

When we got to Yellowstone, we found out the park was closed from a government budget shutdown. So, I never did see a bear on that trip. I had to wait for another trip to Alaska to see a bear in the wild.

But I did get to Idaho and Montana. Plus, we had another great experience, the best Bloody Mary drinks I've ever had. It comes with a story.

When I told my friend Bruce Elder, a lawyer and business professor at UNK, we were going, he said we had to make sure we stopped Dornan's bar and restaurant in Moose, just outside the south entrance to the park. It has a great view of the Tetons and the Snake River, a great deck to view them from and the best Bloody Mary drink.

So, on Sunday morning about 10:30 we rolled into Moose. We went to the front door, asked if they were open. Lunch, no. Bar, yes.

The Bloody Mary was all it had been hyped to be. We decided to call Bruce and to share our experience with him and to find out how he knew about Dornan's. He said that when he was in law school at UNL, one of his classmates lived in Wyoming. They made several trips there so he knew about the place.

"Let me tell you about one of my Bloody Mary stories," he said.

One Friday afternoon, Bruce said he and another young lawyer and business professor Ken Kohrs were driving around Kearney drinking beer in Kohrs car. The car had what they called the 'Dallas Option.' That was an opening in the back seat where they discarded their empty cans. The term came from a whimsical trip to Texas sometime earlier.

"I'm tired of beer," Bruce said that afternoon, "wouldn't a Bloody Mary taste good? I know just where we can get one. Only one problem. It is in Jackson Hole, Wyoming."

Eleven hours later, they arrived. That long drive may be one reason Bruce has always thought those Bloody Mary drinks were so good. And, he is right!

Oh, it might be noted that the trip happened when Bruce or Ken were still single. Otherwise, it might not have happened.

8

Bear-ow, Alaska

Bear-ow, Alaska, n: a polar place

John and Kathy Horvath carved out a career in Alaska after graduating from Kearney State in the 1960s.

They often spent summer time in Nebraska and eventually, after retiring, split their year between Palmer and Kearney.

John played a key role in helping me see my first bear in the wild. But it was different than I had planned. One of the reasons for my passion for seeing those bear was that when a niece got married in Chicago, one of our tourist stops was at the Brookfield Zoo. Their polar bear exhibit got me excited and when I would watch National Geographic television programs I knew I had to see one.

When John and I were together, I would tell him what I wanted to do. John said it wouldn't be a problem. He knew a friend in Barrow, Alaska, who could help us organize a trip in the fall, the best time to see polar bears. This conversation went on for several years. Barrow is the largest city on the North Slope of Alaska above the Arctic Circle. I had this romantic image of flying to Barrow and renting a polar van like the ones I had seen from tour advertisements to Churchill, Canada, a popular polar bear excursion.

I asked John if that was what we would do thinking we would drive to the edge of Barrow to the Arctic Ocean where we would see them on the ice. John's response. "No, we will rent a car and just drive to the dump. They're scavengers, you know."

How devastating.

We never made it to Barrow. Something always came up. Typically, it was weather. John always said it was cheaper to fly to Hawaii than Barrow. Think about it he said, warm Hawaii, or freezing Barrow.

But, in in the summer of 2017, John and Kathy eventually played a key role in my goal to see a bear. With Galen and Marilyn Hadley, Ellen and I made a trip to Alaska. We stayed with the Horvaths before heading to Denali National Park. We were fortunate to have three days of perfect summer weather and saw 13 grizzly bears from our car and a tour bus.

Kathy's career as a teacher has always seemed fascinating. For 14 years during the 1980s and 1990s, she directed correspondence education for the Matanuska-Susitna Burrough, Mat-Su as it was referred to. Kathy was responsible for taking education materials to children who live in the Bush. This required her to reach individual remotely-located homes, not villages who were required to have a school if the village had 8 children.

So, to get to those places, Kathy used every mode of transportation available. She went by dog team, skis, air plane, horses to reach them. Many of those homes were located along the river or near lakes so, she said, it was not unusual to land there when they flew. She would exchange educational materials with the kids, then leave.

She said she remembers one time her pilot came to the house where she was visiting and said to hurry up. A storm was coming and if they didn't leave right away, they might be snowed in for days. As interesting as it sounds, Kathy said that many times going out and coming back, she would be by herself for hours.

9

Vigilante

Vigilante, n: a person who enforces the law
single-handedly, because he has only one arm

When I graduated from college after five years and a couple of summer sessions, I took a job teaching English and journalism at Sidney
High School. One other first year teacher was Dale Butler. We became
fast friends. After a month we moved into a house with two other
teachers.

Dale was born with one arm and part of another. However, that
didn't stop him from being as normal as any person I have ever known.
In college, he lettered in baseball and cross country. He had a love for
all sports. We played a lot of one-on-one basketball in our free time.
Since he had only one arm, I often got by him driving for a layup, but
there also were times when I had bruises from getting the stub in my
side.

As young teachers, we did a lot together. We volunteered for everything – organization sponsors, sports activities helpers and after school
events. Those activities got us invited to monthly poker games with the
older men faculty members.

One of their annual events was a cookout and poker night at a cabin on the North Platte River near Bridgeport, about an hour away.

Dale Butler and me

Sometime during the evening of playing cards, I wandered into the kitchen looking for a snack. I came back with a sandwich. Well, sort of. I slapped two slices of bread together and added popcorn between them.

After the laughter died down, the popcorn sandwich story lived on. The following year and eventually every time I saw a former faculty member, they would ask if I still ate popcorn sandwiches.

More than 35 years later, we got together in Sidney for a day of golf and dinner.

Of course, knowing the popcorn sandwich story would be brought up, I had recipes printed for the 12 who attended.

Popcorn Sandwich Recipe

Two slices of fresh white bread

One bowl of popcorn (individual choice)

Salt to taste

Place popcorn on bottom slice of bread and cover with top slice of bread.

To keep popcorn to keep popcorn from falling out of sandwich, pinch edges of the bread.

If desired, oil can be added

Taste will be enhanced with a drink of one's choice.

One of our first years at Sidney, Dale and I refereed a high school basketball game in Oshkosh for our roommate who had a conflict. I had officiated a lot of high school basketball when I was in college but this was Dale's first game.

For Dale, it was the start of a football and basketball officiating career that spanned more than 45 years. He eventually was inducted into the Nebraska High School Sports Hall of Fame for his work of more than 2,000 games and dedication to developing new, young referees. At the awards ceremony, I marveled at those years of devoted service to one of his passions.

One of my friends when I taught at Kearney State was Wayne Samuelson. He was the basketball coach in the late 1960s and later admissions director. On visits to Kearney, golf with Sam and Dale was a regular part of our social agenda. Sam, who played basketball in college, never excelled at golf even though we played often. He finally gave it up when Butler beat him one handed.

After he left education, Dale embarked on a sales career that began in Norfolk selling metal buildings. That venture got us into a storage building business and eventually other building rental business. One of the things I admired about Dale was his vision and ideas. He also got us into a Mexican fast food franchise business. That wasn't as successful. Probably too much competition from Taco John's and Taco Bell. But, for a while we thought Taco Del Sol was the next major franchise.

The metal building business led to another friendship with Marcus Wacker. When Dale moved from Norfolk, Marcus became a partner in the storage building business. Shortly after that Marcus found an empty seed company building that we purchased. It is now the manufacturing home of MP Global, a company that makes a recycled underlayment for wood flooring.

It has been a very successful business, for MP Global and for our company, Store Safe Inc.

Marcus and his wife, Jean, have a place in Scottsdale and we regularly get together during our stays in Arizona during the winter. Those winter trips would not be complete without regular trips to Turf Paradise for the horse races. Or, as I call it, the Free Money Store.

I tell my friends it works like this - you go up to a window, pick a horse number, give them some money, get a ticket, go out to watch the race, return with your ticket and they give you more money back. Works every time. Well, hardly. Once in a while it does.

The Free Money Store is now part of our vocabulary for a day at the races.

Dale eventually got involved in Subway franchises, owning several. One was on Dodge Street in Omaha, near the University of Nebraska Medical Center.

One lunchtime, a 21-year-old male walked into the restaurant, pulled a knife on an employee, demanded the contents of the cash register and fled.

Dale chased him down.

A story appeared in the *Omaha World-Herald* newspaper as they reported the episode. This is the story.

> Dale Butler didn't think twice. The 60-year-old took off after the robber - tracking him down inside a motel room a block away.
>
> Butler, who was born with one arm, wrestled the man to the ground and held him for police.
>
> Neither his safety nor the money was a concern when he began to chase the man, Butler said.

"I just wanted to catch the little creep," he said.

Although the situation ended without violence, police cautioned citizens against pursuing robbery suspects themselves.

Butler said he was on the telephone in the restaurant's back room when he heard his employee hollering. The employee had just rung up a sandwich and drink order.

"When the drawer come open," Butler said, "the robber pulled out a knife and told her to give him the money."

She stepped back, and the robber reached across the counter and grabbed a handful of money. Then came the hollering.

"I threw down the phone and started chasing him," Butler said.

He followed the man into the Travel Inn motel a block away.

A woman who was nearby told Butler that a man had gone to the second floor. Butler run up the stairs and saw someone leaving an unlocked room.

The man told Butler that the room was empty, but Butler went in anyway.

"That kid in there was trying to change his clothes," Butler said.

Butler grabbed the man and wrestled him down.

Meanwhile, Subway employees had called police.

"I had him well under control by the time they got there. As I was coming out of the room with the guy, the police were in the hallway."

"He didn't think I was going to chase him," Butler said. "If I hadn't chased him, he'd have gotten away with it."

Butler said he subdued the younger man without trouble.

"I'm in pretty darn good shape for my age.

Although the robber didn't make any physical threats, he scared some of the employees, Butler said. "I'd go get him again tomorrow."

After the story appeared in the *World-Herald*, Dale appeared on three Omaha television stations. Several officers came to one of his

Subway shops at noon, during the busiest time of the day and presented him with a crime stopper plaque.

For several years after that event when he was refereeing, fans and coaches would tell him that if they had known he was that tough, they would never have questioned any of his calls.

10

Non-sense

Non-sense, n: logic used by Nonna

For many years, several college friends have gotten together every fall to play golf and socialize in the Fort Collins, Colorado, area where Larry Edwards lives. It's a great several days of reliving our undergraduate days.

We also get together every summer in Kearney for an athletic department fund-raiser golf tournament.

That group is Edwards, Larry Feather, Dave Jones from Colorado; Denny Renter and Dean Osborn from California; and Roger Jones, Jerry Dunlap and me from Nebraska. Those activities have been a fabulous way to spend time together, and share stories and memories of our undergraduate days.

Denny Renter, better known by our group as Boom-Boom for his long drives, left an athletic legacy in college. Denny was a member of the first national team championship.

In 1964, he was a member of the Kearney State bowling team that captured the NAIA Bowling title. Other members were Bernard Mollard, Jon Headrick, Bob Lapp, Dave Sparks and Byron Blobaum.

Headrick, a Phi Tau Gamma fraternity brother of mine, also was the individual national champion.

Larry Feather, Dave Jones, Jerry Dunlap, UNK Athletic
Director Paul Plinske, Burt Bondegard, Denny Renter, Larry
Edwards, Roger Jones

In 2006, that bowling team was honored by UNK athletics as a Team of Distinction.

Well into his 70s, Dean Osborn still plays basketball where he still keeps up with his much younger opponents.

When we get together in the fall, one of our favorite venues has been the Golf Club at Fox Acres in the Red Feather Lakes area near Fort Collins.

It is a wonderful place with cabins for golf, mountain scenery and socializing.

Our outings usually occurred near the time when Fox Acres was closing for the winter, so often we had the place to ourselves.

That meant the staff, often young seasonal help, was ready to go home.

As a group, we would give Dave Jones, a retired banker, money to make one payment for bar tabs, services, tips and things like that.

One year, the staff at Fox Acres was composed of three young college-age women from the Czech Republic.who came to Colorado for summer jobs.

We called them the Czech Chicks.

After a couple of days, we noticed the service was very attentive. It was the same time Dave told us we needed to add money to our kitty.

He said he had been tipping the girls 25 percent which was fine. But it was also on top of the 20 percent gratuity they were already receiving from our automatic billing.

Not a bad deal.

Teasingly, we offered the girls scholarship to stay in the U.S. and come to college at UNK. But, they were ready to go home.

The Czech Chicks will always be one of our fun stories.

At our fall golf outing, we would always start with a cocktail party hosted by Larry Edwards and his wife, Kay.

The question that always came up after one drink was, 'should we have another?' Larry's response has always been, 'We'd be a fool not to.'

All of us have used that phrase in every bar or social setting we have been.

One of eight is Larry Feather, from Grand Junction. We always called him 'Busy' since that is the way he lives. Always on the go.

Feather journals. Especially about golf and his mother-in-law.

His golf journal includes every round, things like fairways hit, greens hit, number of total putts, one putt greens, two putt greens, courses played. He has more statistics than they do on the PGA tour.

For years he journaled the life of his 'beloved mother-in-law Nonna' who lived nearby in Grand Junction until her death at age 94 in 2018. Annually, he would entertain us with some of her stories. All in good taste and with great affection for Nonna.

Among those stories from Feather:

We bought new patio furniture for Nonna's house (which we own) from Sears and paid $800. A few weeks later I noticed an $800 check from my wife Joanna to Nonna. I was told that Nonna didn't like the patio furniture so we bought it from her – thus buying it twice.

Nonna said she would not go out shopping on 'Black Friday' because she was afraid of getting killed.

Four in the morning (not the C&W song by the same name) is when Nonna called me at home and asked me if it was four in the morning or four in the afternoon. I simply told her to look out the window to see if it was daylight or dark. Of course, it was dark.

On being told by the Feather family after a trip to Europe that Rome was expecting 40 million visitors in the year 2000 instead of the normal 15 million, Nonna asked, "I wonder what year it will be there?" I informed Nonna that Rome uses the same calendar as we do.

When telling Larry that when she changes the clocks for daylight savings time, she changes the hour, not the minutes.

On New Year's Eve in 2000, when my wife Joanna asked Nonna why she wasn't wearing her very nice black dress coat to the country club, she said, "I'm afraid it will get stolen."

After Nonna's second bad divorce, husband Russ died, leaving Nonna a $20,000 life insurance payment. I asked Nonna if the insurance company paid her in one lump sum and Nonna said, "No, they sent me a check."

Nonna, commenting on her feet and pointing to them, said, "I've used these feet all my life."

When leaving church one Sunday when it was raining and not opening up her umbrella that she was carrying, Larry asked if she wanted him to open it up for her and she said, "No, I'll save it."

Nonna's daughter-in-law noticed her eating what appeared to be eating a sandwich and simply commented on it. I see you are having a sandwich. Nonna said, "No, it's a piece of bologna in between two pieces of bread."

On a trip to San Francisco while standing on the pier at Fisherman's Wharf, Nonna said, "The altitude here in San Francisco is really affecting me." Nonna's granddaughter, Angie, who was living there at the time said, "We are at sea level and that's the ocean" pointing to the water.

At age 87, Nonna fell in her home, spraining her ankle and bending her glasses. Larry took her to the doctor who asked her what had happened. Nonna said she hit a fake plant but it didn't hurt her face because her glasses broke the fall.

When driving from Manhattan, Kansas, to Topeka with grandson Lucas driving, he noticed Nonna nodding off in the back seat. When she awoke, Lucas asked her if she had a nice nap. Nonna said, "Oh, I wasn't napping. I just had my head down watching the white line on the edge of the highway."

Another time driving across Kansas, we drove by a very large herd of cattle in a large pasture. Several hundred cows by my estimate. Nonna said, "Where do they put all those cows at night? Do the cowboys put them in the barn?" I had no answer.

A few days ago, I adjusted one of Nonna's sprinkler heads hoping to improve the coverage of an area that wasn't getting enough water. I adjusted it so it would do a 360-degree circle. The next day when the water came on, it was hitting the house while Nonna was ironing inside. She called our house and said she was having a storm at her house. I went over to check on the 'storm.' At this point, her neighbor and Nonna were in the back yard in the 'storm' area. Nonna told both of us that when the storm hit, she opened the back door, saw the storm and then told us she was trapped in her own house and couldn't get out because of the storm. I guess she didn't consider using her front door to get away from the storm.

On taking a family picture at Thanksgiving 1999, Nonna hid behind another and said, "I don't want my picture taken until after my surgery." Her surgery was going to be on her foot for a 'hammer toe.'

When Nonna died, she wanted to be remembered as a pie maker. At age 94, she began planning her own funeral. One day, after making arrangements with a local photographer, she baked a banana cream pie and took it down to his studio where he took her picture holding the pie, which she gave him in exchange for the photo. Her plan was that upon her death she wanted have that picture in the paper because she wanted to be remembered as 'the pie lady.'

At her memorial service, guests were served an Italian dinner along with some of her famous cream pies. The pies were prepared by a local baker that had gotten Nonna's recipe from Larry's wife, Nonna's daughter Joanna.

The only problem was the pie crusts were almost impossible to cut. Joanna told the pie story to the group with a huge smile. "I know my mom is looking down saying 'I told you I was the best pie maker!'"

11

Dig'naught'ary

Dig'naught'ary, n: a person who does not hold a high office but is bestowed with a title

In 2003 I created an 'honorary doctorate degree' for Larry that we presented one evening after golf and dinner at Fox Acres Country Club in Red Feather Lakes. I had called my daughter Tracy, who majored in French, to help me with a title for the degree. She had the perfect insight – mouche du coche.

Here is my explanation of the degree:

The honorary degree 'The Great Mouche Du Coche' is a famous French term. United States colleges and universities have used the elegant French language as the source of many honorary doctorate degree titles for centuries. The French traditionally have been able to capture the true essence of a simple phrase with dignity and class that no other language is capable of. Having an honorary degree with a French title is a prized possession among those in the educated world. Colleges and universities go to great lengths to pick the precise words for such a degree knowing that, in most cases, they are singular in their presentation. This degree is the only one of its kind known to exist. Thus, the person possessing this degree will stand above the rest.

The term 'mouche du coche' means busybody, certainly a term that is appropriate to our recipient. Separately, 'mouche' is a French term for 'fly' and 'coche' is an 'auto' or 'coach.' Thus, the literal meaning is 'a fly that bounces from car to car.'

There was nobody prouder of an award than the new 'Dr Feather' was when it was presented. He took it home, had it framed and hung it in his office. He also keeps a photocopy in his car and always has an extra one to show anybody interested. He told us a few years ago that at a hospital board meeting he almost got tripped up when someone on the board asked him what kind of doctor he was. He got out by saying 'honorary' before the topic of conversation changed.

Naturally, since that presentation, he will forever be known as Dr. Feather. Or, to complicate matters, maybe Doctor, Admiral Feather.

In 2015, as Nebraska senator and speaker of the Nebraska Legislature, Galen Hadley was acting governor when both the governor and lieutenant governor were out of the state. As acting governor, Speaker Hadley conferred a special title on each of us – Admiral in the Great Navy of the State of Nebraska. Everybody received one at our annual fall golf outing.

This is the history of the honor:

It is Nebraska's highest honor, perhaps even the highest honor in the U.S., since Nebraska is the only triply landlocked state, requiring travel through three states to reach an ocean, gulf, or bay. The honorary title is bestowed upon individuals by approval of the Governor of Nebraska. It is not a military rank, requires no duties, and carries with it no pay or other compensations.

The certificate describes the honor in a tongue-in-cheek fashion:

And I (the Governor of Nebraska) do strictly charge and require all officers, seamen, tadpoles and goldfish under your command to be obedient to your orders as Admiral – and you are to observe and follow, from time to time, such directions as you shall receive, according to the rules and discipline of the Great Navy of the State of Nebraska.

The use of the title 'Admiral,' instead of some other high-ranking military title, is a humorously ironic reference to the fact that Nebraska has no navy, both because has no oceans, seas or major lakes to defend, and because it relies on the United States Armed Forces for defense and has had no active state defense since 1972.

The Great Navy of the State of Nebraska was created in 1931. The Lieutenant Governor at the time, Theodore W. Metcalfe, was serving as acting governor while 20 to 25 prominent Nebraskans were named as Nebraska Admirals.

The tradition of awarding 'admiralships' is a popular recognition at special events regularly.

12

Flinty-foolery

Flinty-foolery, n: yabba dabba doings

When I was in college in the early 1960s, I lived in a dormitory, a fraternity house, an apartment and finally a house with four other friends, a place that became known as the Flinty House. That term evolved from an intramural basketball team I played on, called the Flintstones, after giving up a dream to play college basketball.

Not to be confused with an Honor's Hall, the Flinty House became a popular place for weekend parties and gatherings.

At the time, the university had standards for approved off campus housing. Of course, we didn't meet any of those standards. Among those were a bed for each person living there and a study desk for everyone. We didn't have a bed in the two-bedroom house. Nor, did we have a desk. We did have a hide-a-bed in one bedroom

Jerry Dunlap, me, Doug Glascock

and two single mattresses in the other bedroom along with a couch in the living room.

The friendships that developed from that year have lasted.

13

Mayor

Mayor, n: a job with varied responsibilities

Roger Jones was one of the four. He had been president of his fraternity and a member of student council. He got around. Even though
he was enrolled in college, early in the fall of 1963, Roger got drafted.
It was Vietnam War time. The night before he had to leave, we had a
party to send him off then took him to the bus depot in his home town
of Minden, twenty miles away, for the trip to Omaha where he was to
take his army physical.

When we arrived in Minden, parents were sending their sons off
with a lot of tears. As Roger's buddies, we pleaded with the bus driver
not to take him and even lay in front of the bus in a mock protest. To
no avail. Roger left and we returned to college that morning.

Three days later, who shows up back in Kearney? Roger Jones. He
failed his physical because of a hearing defect. Actually, he had an ear
infection. It was another reason to celebrate. Later, he was recalled for
another induction physical, but by then he had a college student defer-
ment.

Roger has remained at the top of my inner circle for 50 years. When
I was alumni director, I talked Roger into serving on the board of di-

rectors. His career at the time was serving as a sales rep for Vanity Fair Company selling Lee Jeans. He eventually became alumni association president. Then he served on the Kearney State College Foundation Board of Directors and was hired as executive vice president of the Foundation continuing when it merged with the University of Nebraska Foundation, a position he held until he retired.

Roger Jones, me, John Horvath, Tom Wisdom, Dave Klone, Kent Mattson, Doug Glascock

A consummate joiner of nearly every organization imaginable, he has served as a councilman and mayor of his home town, Minden.

When Roger was elected mayor in 2008, he defeated a person whose job was grounds keeper for the Minden Public Schools. Roger's mother-in-law, Gladys, who was 91 years old at the time, told Roger's wife, Rita, that she didn't know how Roger would be able to handle the job as mayor. "Rita, how is Roger going to mow all those yards? He doesn't even mow his own yard."

One thing has never changed since college. Roger loves Coors beer. His favorite line has always been, "How they can make it so good, ship it so far and sell it so cheap is beyond me."

We have played golf together for years, traveled socially and worked tirelessly for the university in our professional work.

14

Political ties

Political ties, n: dinner and ice cream with the governor

Kent Mattson was another of the Flinty House roommates. After he graduated, he and his wife, Jane, had a career as teachers in Kenai, Alaska. I was always fascinated at how Kent survived the Alaska dark winters and the teacher's schedule of getting up in the morning. Getting up early was not a quality I remember him having at the Flinty House. I even saw it first-hand even living with Kent and his family in southern California the summer before we moved into the Flinty House.

It took Kent an inordinate amount of time to do most things, more than most people. One of those was playing golf. Kent had a putter cover that he would take off and put on after every hole. It took time, a lot of time. One of our friends, John Horvath, who was playing with us one day said he had a nightmare that woke him up. "I had dreamt that Kent got covers for all his golf clubs," John said.

Kent attended UNL his freshman year of college where he was a fraternity pledge brother of Bob Kerrey, who later became Nebraska governor and U.S. senator from Nebraska.

The summer Kerrey was running for governor in 1982, Kent and Jane came back from Alaska for the summer. He asked if that was the same Bob Kerrey he knew. Which it was.

The next summer after Kerrey was elected, Kent called him to wish him well. Kerrey invited Kent and Jane to visit him at the governor's mansion before they went back north. Kent and Jane, along with their two young daughters, drove to Lincoln, checked into the Cornhusker Hotel before walking several blocks to the governor's mansion.

When Kent and Jane arrived, they rang the doorbell and were greeted by the maid. "We are Kent and Jane Mattson," they said. "Come in," she said, "the governor is expecting you."

Just then, Debra Winger, actress and the governor's girlfriend, came running down the stairs. "Hi, I'm Debra." Bob was right behind her.

They had met when Debra was in Lincoln filming part of the Oscar-winning movie, *Terms of Endearment.*

That movie had additional significance since in it, Debra's husband, Flap, takes a position as head of the English Department at Kearney State College. Rather than shoot part of the film in Kearney, it was shot on campuses in Lincoln.

"We have a surprise for you," the governor said to Kent and Jane on seeing them that evening. "Debra is fixing dinner for us tonight."

During the spaghetti dinner, Governor Kerrey asked Kent about his family. Kent and Jane told about their two daughters and that they were at the Cornhusker Hotel.

"Let's go get them and have some ice cream," Kerrey said.

They picked up the girls, Katie and Stacy, and went to Baskin-Robbins near the UNL campus. "You can imagine the crowd there on a hot summer night. The governor, Debra Winger and us," Kent said.

Of course, as Kent remembered, nobody hardly cared about the governor. But Debra was another matter. The same was true when they went to their old fraternity house just a few blocks away.

After they retired, Kent and Jane would spend their summers in Alaska and return to Nebraska in the fall. Both were huge Cornhusker football fans.

Coming home late from a game November 12, 2009, they swerved to miss a deer on Interstate 80 near Aurora and were hit from behind by a semi. Both were killed in the accident. They are my closest friends that I have lost and have left a huge void in my life. That death did illustrate how fragile life is and how important it is to pursue your dreams and enjoy your family and friends and every day of your life.

15

Roommates

Roommates, n: experiences in college living

Doug Glascock also was a Flinty House roommate. We lived together three years while in college. When I think back, I have trouble remembering how all of us got to be such good friends.

It could have started when we were in elementary school playing baseball together.

In college we were in different fraternities and had different majors. Doug and I came from North Platte but I had gone to catholic school and Doug to public school. And, we were not in the same class. He started out at UNL where he was on the freshman football team as a running back. But he left after one semester and transferred to Kearney.

The year we lived in the Flinty House, we shared myriad experiences. Doug was a great accounting student and one of the nicest guys on campus. That's why this story is memorable. For a sorority formal dance, Doug had a first date with a young co-ed arranged by one of her sorority sisters. It seemed perfect. Doug certainly was a gentleman and would fit in perfectly. One of his friends, Denny Lienemann, dated a girl in the same sorority and they decided to double date for the dance.

Early in the afternoon, Denny and Doug started 'happy hour' to get ready for the dance. By dance time, they were definitely 'in the cups' as the saying goes.

About 10 o'clock that evening, the front door to our house opened and Doug walked in. First, he slammed the door shut, breaking a window. Then he explained his early arrival back home. During a break in the dance, one of the girls got pinned. As was tradition, all of the sorority girls got in a circle to sing their song. Right in the middle of the ceremony, Doug knocked over a table with drinks and food, falling to the floor, barely able to get up. It disrupted the ceremony abruptly. One of the dance sponsors and sorority advisers came over and said, "Son, you've had way too much to drink. I think you need to go home." A friend drove him home. What was a perfect 'blind date' for a big occasion ended in less than a desirable way.

After he graduated, Doug went to work for Enron where he eventually became CFO of one of their divisions, first in Omaha and later in Houston. He left the company before its downfall.

He had a successful accounting career following that.

In his younger days, Doug was never particular about what he ate. It was not unusual for him to open a can of almost anything and eat it right out of the can – soup, spaghetti, dog food. When I was first married, Doug came to Kearney to spend the weekend with us. Lynn had made pea soup that we didn't finish eating and just suck it back in the refrigerator. A day or so later, she knew she would throw it out as it had acquired some mold. After a Saturday evening of celebrating, Doug went to the refrigerator to look for something to eat. Everyone else was in bed. Pea soup fit the bill, mold and all.

The next morning Doug complained of not feeling well, probably due to the soup.

Not to worry though. We loaded him up with a couple of cans of soup for his trip back home to Omaha. Naturally, he ate them along the way.

We had a common friend, Dan Christensen, growing up in North Platte who graduated from the Kansas City Art Institute and became a highly successful abstract artist in New York City. He is best known for paintings that relate to lyrical abstraction, color field painting and abstract expressionism. His works are a part of major national and international collections such as the Chicago Art Institute and Metropolitan Museum of Art, along with the Museum of Nebraska Art in Kearney.

Dan died in 2007 at the age of 64. Doug bought a couple of his paintings from a gallery in New Mexico. When he acquired the paintings, he called to tell me that he bought one after the gallery owner said Dan's works were very high quality and of course he wasn't going to be doing any more. Doug said he paid more for that first painting that he did for his first house. On the way home from the gallery, Doug decided to buy another smaller piece. I guess that is what happens when you are a successful accountant and don't have children.

Doug and I played golf often during our college days. I remember one of his favorite lines.

Before metal drivers, Doug used to always say this about his golf game. "I'm hitting the woods good. I just can't get out of them."

16

Entertaining

Entertaining, v: whistling while you work and play

That last year of college while living in the Flinty House, I also was editor of the student newspaper, *The Antelope*.

When some student brought in a notice of an annual spring talent show sponsored by his student fine art honorary organization, I got an idea about something we could do.

I had just seen a story about another college group who had put together a skit based on the movie, *The Bridge on the River Kwai*. That 1957 World War II movie featured POWs marching and whistling the movie's theme song.

We can do that I told my roommates Doug and Roger. Let's give it a shot. So, we did.

We found six friends who also thought it sounded fun.

The costumes were something like this.

We needed to make paper mache helmets to begin with. That required chicken wire which we acquired through a midnight requisition from the theater department.

The chicken wire was used to create helmets that were about three feet in diameter, formed to cover our heads and faces. Out arms were folded above our heads into the helmets. The helmets were painted army green.

Then we painted our bodies like faces – eye rings around our breasts, a nose in the middle of our stomach and different shapes of mouths around our belly buttons. That created the faces.

On the lower part of our bodies we wore army shirts that covered our legs and hung to the shoes.

One of the guys painted his face black to give us some diversity, a term we really didn't understand then.

The idea was that we would be like the prisoners in *The Bridge on the River Kwai*. We would march on stage sucking our stomachs in and out to the whistling tune from the movie, making it look like we were doing the whistling.

COLLEGE   **PUBLICATION**

KEARNEY STATE COLLEGE   Friday, February 28, 1964

YENRAEK TROUP
The Yenraek Troup, doing a carryoff of "Bridge On The River Kwi" won second place in the novelty division of the K-Show.

It was great fun. I think if we had spent as much time on our class work as we did on this skit, we could have made the dean's list. Or, for most of us, graduate on schedule.

The performance went well. We won a cash prize of $10. Ours was a nice change of pace from the other acts that included singers, piano players, a baton twirler, magicians, comedians, dancers and things like that.

17

Tech WIZard

**Tech WIZard, n: a person using technology
in innovative ways**

Neither Tom Wisdom 'Wiz' nor I can remember how we met
nearly 60 years ago.

We were both from North Platte, but that is the extent of it.

He is three years younger, moved there when he was a junior in
high school and I was in college. We went to different high schools and
in college we were in different fraternities and social groups.

One connection was my roommate Doug Glascock, also from North
Platte. Several evenings during the fall, Doug and I would pick Tom up,
drive around and drink a quart of beer. Then we would head to a favorite college late-night diner called Little USA for two eggs, toast and
hash browns. All for $1.59. Tom and I talk about those nights like they
were yesterday.

We both did have an interest in golf. Tom played freshman football,
but gave that up and played on the golf team. That could have been the
hook that kept us as friends.

Eventually, Tom went off to teach high school math and coach. I
came back to Kearney State to teach. Tom spent his summers in Kear-

ney where we reconnected. Tom met Judy Johnson and married her on June 17, 1972. I was honored to serve as best man.

Tom and Judy Wisdom

Through the years I followed the athletic, personal and professional careers of their three sons. The youngest, Ty, and his wife, Crystal, are my most regular friends during our winter stay in the Phoenix area where Ty is a teacher and football coach, and Crystal is a nurse.

During the COVID 19 issues and self-distancing in the summer of 2020, Wiz was driving around Lexington one afternoon when he saw several older women social distancing several feet apart while they visited with one another in one of their driveways. Even though he didn't know them, Wiz stopped, rolled down his window and said, "I'll bet a bottle of wine would really taste good right now."

"No, one replied, but a rootbeer float certainly would."

Wiz laughed, left and returned shortly after that with root beer floats for all of them.

It was vintage Tom Wisdom and small town friendliness.

Much of my time now is trying to figure out Tom's text messages. He has one of the last flip phones around so in trying to text, his keyboard is a bit difficult to navigate.

In trying to get together recently, I called him to check on their availability. He first texted, 'Wats the program' probably wondering what we were going to do. I texted, 'Coming over?' Later he texted back, 'Plan' – no punctuation, nor comment.

Or, how about, "Call when time.' Probably wanted me to get in touch with him.

A simple phone call worked much better. His kids say they don't even try to read his texts. They just call their mother, Judy.

Instead of calling Siri on his flip phone, an impossibility, Tom simply opens his phone, holds it to his mouth and says, 'Judy.' He then asks her the question most people would ask Siri.

I also am always amused when Tom calls to ask me his wife Judy's favorite wine. Tom, it's J. Lohr cabernet.

18

Believe

Believe, adj: sometimes it's hard to

Another Flinty House roommate when I was a senior in college was Wayne Daugherty. Wayne was exceptionally creative and bright. He started his college career at the U.S. Air Force Academy and finished at Kearney State College.

Wayne died in October 2019, taking his own life at age 75.

His obituary, obviously self-written, touches on some of that creativity.

Stuart Wayne Daugherty

October 24, 1943 – October 1, 2019

So Wayne went Kerflooey and that's it.

If details are wanted, then here. Wayne Daugherty, formerly of Johnson Lake, NE, went Kerflooey on October 1, 2019 at his home in Hot Springs, AK.

Wayne was born Stuart Wayne Daugherty on October 24, 1943 in Washington DC to Ivan Glen and Vivian Iola (Blevins) Daugherty. He graduated from Lexington High School and received his MBA from Kearney State College.

Wayne was married to Dolly DeMoss on June 8, 1967. Wayne was a salesman, English teacher, guidance counselor, businessman and retired person. He read more books than quite possibly any other living person. He loved to tinker with projects in his workshop and spending time with family.

Wayne is survived by his wife, Dolly, daughter Liz (Dave) Bushey of Bennington, NE, son Adam and fiancé Tracey Johnson of Elwood, NE; grandson, Joseph Bushey, granddaughter, Lea Bushey; sisters, Linda (Bill) Behn and Cindy Daugherty; brother, Kenneth Daugherty; and many nieces and nephews.

Wayne was preceded in death by his parents and brother, Dale Daugherty.

If you knew him, lucky you; or not. If you remember him, thank you. And when the last person who remembered him is gone, so then will he really be gone and forgotten. Until then get on with your lives. Please and thank you.

When we were in college, Wayne wrote a column titled 'Hard to Believe,' for the student newspaper.

He also wrote some ad copy for the Mill's Men's clothing store where he worked. The ad copy was similar to a column with just his written message. They were among the most popular and widely read parts of the paper.

One he wrote was:

I greeted my Boss as he was hanging up some sport coats.

"What in blazers is going on here?" I said, barely able to keep from laughing at my own sense of humor.

"Keep it up you mirthless bum," my boss replied, "and I'll see to it that you never guffaw with this company.'"

I could tell I was in for a battle of the minds, and I was hoping my Boss didn't have anything to fight wit.

"Why don't you jus' sleeve me alone, Boss" I asked.

"Leave me alone," I yelled belting him in the waist.

"Don't you mean Levi alone? he chortled.

"What ever started this inseamly argument?" I pleaded.

"If you ask me that question one more time I'll sock you, he said.

I knew he had me collared. I hadn't sized him up properly. It looked like he would kick me on the button, "throw me out the store. One last chance I decided, and . . .

"A stitch in time saves nine, Boss," I began. "Let's mend our disagreement and stop having fits about nothing."

"Sew what, Twirp," he replied briefly.

"You're one of the biggest sweaters I know, Boss," I panted. "Let's just give up the whole thing for lint."

But he wasn't about to quit, so I knocked him unconscious with a hard finish dress trouser. When the police came they arrested me for assault and battery and put me in a dry cell.

"I hereby sentence you to five years in the iron, Mills," the judge said. "Bring on the next witness. This case is clothed."

Another favorite:

"Good morning, Sir Twirp," my boss screamed. Actually I think he intended to say, "Twirp, Sir," because I know he's trusted and respected me ever since I told him I was supporting a wife and two hungry children on the small, but insufficient, paycheck I received each week, although he doesn't trust me and refuses to respect me because I won't tell him whose wife I'm supporting.

"Good morning, Boss," I responded eagerly.

"This is no time for sarcasm, Twirp," my boss said, sarcastically. "We need a catchy little slogan for the store. Something that will become an inherent part of everyones stockpile of catchy little slogans."

Luckily, I had anticipated his request after he ordered me to come up with some catchy little slogans over the weekend.

"Well then," I suggested, cunningly revealing my catchiest slogan first in order to catch him off guard. "How about, 'Buy your clothes at Mills.'"

I could tell I had caught him off guard. "It stinks," he said bitterly.

"Well then," I suggested, resorting to second best. "How about, 'From mountain plains to widest hills the man who cares buys clothes at Mills.'"

"Is that the best you have to offer, Twirp?" My boss demanded.

I hurried on, heedless of criticism. "Do you like saving money, collecting dollar bills? Then grab your dough, get up and go, conserve cash at Mills!"

"Bah Humbug," my boss cried, falling into the spirit of things.

Actually, I can't explain what happened next. Suffice it to say that if you know anyone who can use a well-trained, full time twirp, call 7-3658 any time after classes or on April 13. I'll be there.

One ad he wrote was under the simple headline,

A SUBTLE AD

It's not like we were trying to kid you about things. Let's face it. This is an advertisement. Its purpose is not to entertain, but to bring untold numbers of customers to our store. With money. To spend. On clothes.

We realize that not everything a man learns at college is taught in the classroom. For instance, do you recall the last time your English teacher told you about the new Ban-Lon shirts at our store? For that matter, do you remember your English teacher?

I thought not. So, skip your next English class and hurry to our store. With money. To spend. On clothes. Buy a Ban-Lon.

Wear it back to school. Wear it to the Dean's office when he calls you in to ask about your skips. He'll be impressed. Your folks will be impressed when you get kicked out of school for skipping classes, too. But you'll have your Ban-Lon. And your green stamps. If you can remember, tell people where you got them. At Mills. In Kearney. Downtown.

Wayne's columns reflected his sense of humor, too. This one was printed under the headline, "The Weekly Whether Report."

To paraphrase some poet or another, "Breathes there a man with soul so dead, who never to himself hath said, Hey, check out the dolly."

Which brings us, hard as it is to believe, to our subject: Snow Jobs.

As any self-respecting college student knows, snow jobs are an inherent part of everybody's education. The male student is award that the female student is not going to take the initiative and ask him for a date. He must, therefore, devote some thought to sufficiently impress his prospective date so that when he does ask her out, she will accept without hesitation or any show of negative emotion. This task is usually the simplest part of his problem, since neither the boy or the girl is really sure what the other is like until they have actually spent an evening together. The real difficulty arises when he asks her for another date. Has he conducted himself in a fashion agreeable to his date? Agreeable enough, in fact, to insure acceptance of another offer on his part.

In order to expedite campus romances, the following types of snow jobs are listed in the hope that (1) they will be used, (2) in the event they are not used the female will at least know what she is missing, and (3) that I never date a girl who has read the list. After all, why waste time on someone who knows exactly what I might say, and more frightening, might say it first.

The first and most common type of snow job is simple and direct flattery, i.e., "Dear you're the best thing that ever happened to me. Without you I'd just be another face in the crowd. Etc. etc. etc." Although it may be corny, it sometimes works, (or so I'm told).

If, however, it doesn't work, don't give up hope. The second type of snow job of note is as follows: Be brisk and businesslike in your approach, adopting an attitude of "I love you, naturally, but I have other obligations to attend to." Don't say this by all means, just give the impression. A suggested vocalization of this line might be, "I have neither the time nor the talent to snow you, so you are going to have to snow me." If your date takes you seriously, give yourself 10 points. If she doesn't take you seriously, at least she'll think you're witty. At any rate you haven't lost any ground.

Although you haven't lost any ground, you haven't gained any either. Try this, "Dearest, you deserve nothing but the best," (Pause to let her absorb the preceding.) Follow closely with, "And I'm the best there is." If she doesn't think you're egotistical, crude and arrogant, you're in a good position to forge onward. If she does, however, sense that you're just kidding, quickly pull a reverse as follows: "I'm sorry which although it is meaningless will confuse the issue so that you can move on to the next step.

By now, your date should be ecstatic. She should be snowed. If she isn't then either, (1) forget it and get another girl, (2) forget it because you can't, get another girl, (3) turn on her hearing aid and start over.

The preceding helpful hints should be more than sufficient to snow even the most cold-hearted senior, but sometimes it requires this last-ditch effort. If this final attempt is a failure, turn in your badge and join a monastery; and you might not succeed there.

This is my own line. I have devoted months of intense effort to develop the perfect snow-job. Without exception, it has not failed when used properly. I hesitate to release it to the public, but I shall do so, for if one person benefits from my efforts, I shall be happy, knowing I have done my bit for humanity and the snow-job.

(continued on page 5)

That week *The Antelope* published only four pages.

One winter night, we arrived home to the Flinty House about midnight and opened the front door to a living room filled with smoke.

Wayne was asleep on the couch, his nightshirt smoldering along with the middle cushion of our three-cushion couch. A partially smoked Winston cigarette was nearby.

We woke Wayne, got him out of his night shirt and threw the still-smoldering cushion out the front door on a small snow bank. It could have been a major disaster, but fortunately ended okay.

We lived the rest of the semester with a couch that had only two cushions. When we moved out that spring, we took the couch, along with some other furnishing to the local Paul Londer weekly auction. The couch brought $2.50. The leftover chicken wire from our 'The Bridge on the River Kwai' skit brought $10.

One spring day, a US Air Force representative official showed up at our door looking for Wayne. Wayne had been a student at the Air Force Academy as a freshman before leaving after the first semester.

The reason for the visit, we learned later, was that as a cadet who accepted an appointment to the academy, Wayne had a military commitment to complete. Now, four years later, he had had no communication with the Air Force. He had not answered any of their letters or communications. So, they wanted to talk to him about his military obligation.

After being told Wayne was working at Mill's Clothing in downtown Kearney, the gentleman proceeded there to find him.

Upon entering Mill's, the official met a salesman and said he was looking for Wayne. The response was, 'Wayne left earlier.' Of course, the official was talking to Wayne.

The official just shook his head. "I don't know what is going on. I don't know whether Wayne Daugherty even exists. I can't find him anywhere. Maybe he is a ghost. Maybe you are him. I just want to get this issue cleared up. He has been assigned to a reserve unit for four years but he has never attended or responded to any communication. He needs to take care of his responsibility."

The guy left without any satisfaction.

Sometime later Wayne got another letter from the US Air Force. It was his official discharge from the service.

In 1990, Wayne was president to the UNK Alumni Association.

At the time, Wayne was in the business phase of his career. He was a vice president of the Buckle Corporation, a clothing store chain for young adults that had its headquarters in Kearney. The company had fewer than 100 stores with plans to continue expansion.

One of the concerns was developing a more sophisticated distribution center. However, Wayne said the Buckle brought in an expert in distribution, but his fee was quite high. So Wayne explored other possibilities.

As alumni president, Wayne traveled with the Alumni Association to various gatherings around the country. One of those was an early February event in Southern California.

Since we had one morning free, Wayne make a contact with a company called Clothestime. Clothestime was a retailer of sportswear on the west coast with had more than 200 stores in the early 1990s. They also had a distribution center in Anaheim, where we were staying.

Wayne took me with him to look at their distribution center. After we got done with our visit and tour, Wayne said their setup was just what the Buckle was looking at. When we returned to Kearney, Wayne designed the major development of a new distribution center, saving the company a huge amount of money.

19

Sidney Support

Sidney Support, n: loyalty through hard times

When I went to Sidney to teach in 1964, I ran into a friend that I had known briefly in college, Jody Haugan. He became a special person in my life. Some of my fondest and my saddest memories are tied to our friendship.

Jody was married to Susie and worked for her father in a very successful grocery store, Town and Country Market. Susie, bless her heart, was 18 years old, but served in many capacities for Jody's friends. She would do things like fix us dinner, let us hang out at their house to watch football or whatever sporting event was on, or just let us be part of their lives.

I think Jody was a little jealous of my freedom and my teaching job, but I was equally jealous of him for having a nice house, a Chevrolet convertible and what seemed like an idyllic life. For the three years I lived in Sidney, he was as much of a brother to me as my own brothers were.

I left Sidney in 1967 to return to graduate school at Kansas State University. When I got married that next June to a girl from Sidney,

Jody was part of the wedding. He and Susie visited us that summer in Manhattan, Kansas, as I finished my master's degree, and that fall when I started teaching at the University of Nebraska in Kearney.

Shortly after that, Jody and Susie's marriage started to unravel. He eventually purchased the grocery store in 1988 from Susie's parents but couldn't make it work. He drank too much and didn't handle the business well which he eventually lost after a divorce and alcohol-related events.

By that time, his ex-wife Susie had moved to Phoenix with their two children. She had $5,000, no education and the kids. She made a life for herself with a dedication to hard work.

Jody continued to spiral downward.

We used to invite him to Kearney for a few days. If his car worked, he would come. If not, he would stay in Sidney. A person with untold friends, he did odd jobs for them but eventually he cut corners on such things as painting and landscaping overbilling for work he didn't finish. Although everyone was willing to help him, those relationships collapsed. Jody spent time in alcohol rehab, and faced related health issues that caused a stroke.

This was from a man who at one time had a new Chevy convertible and a pickup.

His last trip to visit us was memorable because of how things had changed in his life.

I gave him directions to our house that were relatively simple. Get off I-80 at exit 272 (Kearney), go north to 25th Street, left to Country Club Lane, then right to our house. Since he had been to Kearney in the past and had gone to college here where he was on the golf team, he was familiar with the city.

When he got here, he called and said he couldn't find us. He had simply gotten off the interstate, and turned south and pulled over. He did have his dad's cell phone. I gave him directions again. Ten minutes later, he said he couldn't find our house. Through a series of questions, I was still at a loss. Jody, I said, what can you remember after you called me? He said all he could remember was going under that decorative overpass which turned out to be the Great Platte River Archway Monument. He had gotten back on the interstate and taken the next exit where he pulled over again and called. The only sign he saw was Highway 10. We eventually found him and drove him to our house where he stayed for a couple of days. I think Lynn and I were his last true friends. When it was time to go back to Sidney, I took him to Interstate 80, pointed him west and told him not to get off until he got to Sidney.

His death February 10, 2006, at age 65 was difficult to accept. I had been a part of his early success and sadly watched him lose his way and destroy himself.

20

Venturas

**Venturas, n: adventures with the athletic
director of Ventura College**

When I was a freshman in college, my path crossed that of Jerry
Dunlap. He played football and I was on the freshman basketball team.

As sophomores, Jerry talked me into going to the class meeting at
the beginning of the school year. He said it would be a good way to
meet girls. I can't remember meeting anyone new, but Jerry was elected
president and I was elected vice president of the sophomore class.

By the time we were seniors, we had experienced most of the joys of
college.

One night at a party during Christmas vacation, we ran low on beer.
Jerry had his first car of his college life, a 1954 Chevy convertible. It
was really nice. Jerry and I headed down Fifth Avenue in Kearney to a
liquor store on slick roads caused by an earlier snow. Fortunately, the
icy roads meant everyone was driving slowly, including us.

At the intersection of Fifth Avenue and U.S. Highway 30 that ran
though Kearney, we slid through the stop sign and were broadsided by
an oncoming truck, also going slow. The impact spun us around, only
to be banged into again by the truck. The good news was neither of us

spilled the beer we were carrying. The other good news was the car was drivable.

The next day, I went with Jerry to get an estimate on the damages. We pulled up to a repair shop in downtown Kearney, got out, walked in with our problem. The owner of the shop grabbed his pen and followed us outside. He took one look at the car and said to Jerry, "Son, from the front bumper to the door on the driver's side, the car is a total loss." We thanked him, got in and drove off. Jerry drove the car the rest of the year.

After Jerry graduated in 1963, he moved to Brawley, California, where he taught and coached for three years. He returned to Kearney State in 1966 where he served as a graduate assistant while earning a master's degree.

Jerry returned to California in 1n 1967 where he embarked on a distinguished career in education, including more than 30 years as athletic director at Ventura College.

The day he left, he stopped at my home in North Platte, to say goodbye. I had another year of college to finish so wasn't going any place. In our farewell, Jerry took a one-dollar bill from his billfold, tore it in half and wrote Jim R and Jerry D on each half. More than 50 years later, I still carry my half in my billfold. It has always been a reminder of our friendship.

One of my great honors was serving as best man when he married Mary Manlein in 1966. He had returned to Kearney State to be a graduate assistant earlier that year. After he graduated with a master's degree that spring, Jerry and Mary moved back to California. I visited them often when I was alumni director since we had a strong Southern California alumni club.

Every summer Jerry, Mary and their two children would return to Nebraska to visit family and friends. He always brought me Ventura College workout gear.

In 1976, after one such visit, I wrote him a letter of thank you. Of course, it wasn't just a simple letter, it was more of a quirky message that shows I had too much time on my hands. I included a picture I had taken with the workout gear while holding a basketball.

November 17, 1976

Dear Basketball Coach,

I just wanted to thank you for the basketball scholarship your athletic director gave me last summer when he was in Nebraska and apologize for not showing up for classes the first semester of this year. I will be coming for second semester and will be ready to begin playing.

If Mr. Dumlap didn't tell you about me this letter will help. I have been out of high school for a couple of years working and trying to find the right place to play collage ball. After the recruiting pitch by Mr. Dumlap I know Ventura is the right place for me. He watched me play last summer and said that he new I could play for you. I am sending a pitcher of myself. I have been practicing as much as possible to get ready for you in fact right now I am playing in a local leage. In high scool I made 28 points a game. Mr. Dumpap said he thot that was very good when he recruited me. I am 6-foot high but I like to play in the cornur where you can get those good jump shoots that is my best shot.

How much collage class work do I gotta take? I didn't do real good in high scool but that was caus many of my teachers didn't like me. I will do good in collage tho. Right and tell me what I shuld take.

Be sure to tell Mr. Dumlap how much I appreciated The scholarship he give me and the bounes for coming to your collage. Also let me no what I shuld be working on and where will I live when I get there, also how I get there.

See you in Janrary.

Seneurly,
Jim Rundstrom

Jerry made friends fast and always had connections.

When Pope John Paul II came to the United States in 1987 one of his stops was in Los Angeles. Jerry engaged his good friend and former pastor Monsignor Terrance Fleming to get him involved in the pope's visit. By the pope's visit time, Father Terry had become a monsignor, who then lived in LA. He was coordinator of the pope's Southern California stop.

Jerry's job was to carry what he called the 'bribe bag,' for monsignor Terry. A typical task was for Monsignor Terry to approach somebody with a need they had for the pope's mass at the Los Angeles Coliseum. For example, if they needed a sound system, Monsignor Terry would trade special tickets to the mass for the sound system. That mass attracted a crowd of 103,000. After the pope left, Jerry was able to acquire many things that were left in the pope's room at the catholic rectory – bottles of wine, blessed rosaries, and all types of catholic memorabilia. Jerry gave my mother, a devout catholic, a rosary blessed by the pope. It was one of her most prized possession.

In 1996, Jerry got a volunteer job at the Atlanta Olympics through some connections in California. His connection was with the company that provided the floor for the basketball and gymnastics arena.

My daughter, Tracy, who was a college student at TCU, also had a volunteer position. I drove her to Atlanta and left a car for her for the two weeks of the Olympics. Then I flew home.

While I was in Atlanta, Jerry and I got together one day. He had been there for a week before the Olympics started so by the time Tracy and I arrived, Jerry was ready to do something different than just hang around the Olympic site.

I suggested the Atlanta zoo, one of my favorites that I had visited twenty years earlier. Located in Grant Park, there was a cyclorama and Civil War Museum that depicted the Battle of Atlanta led by General Sherman.

Jerry and I found a city bus that took us to Grant Park. When we got there, we were early and nothing was open yet, so we decided to find place to have coffee. No such luck. After walking around for a while, we went to the zoo offices and asked them where we could find coffee. The young lady we talked to at the zoo office said she didn't think there was anything close by within walking distance. Just before we left, she said, "Hey, why don't you just come back to our break room. We have coffee and rolls."

Naturally, our conversation turned to why we were there. Jerry said we were working at the Olympics but need a break so we came to the zoo. I remembered one of the zoo's main attractions, a gorilla named Willie B who, at the time, was the star attraction. Willie B came to the zoo when he was small and lived until 2000 when he died at age 42.

While we were having coffee, the zoo director Dr. Terry Maple came in and stopped by for a short visit. We knew just enough about the zoo that we could carry on a conversation with Dr. Maple especially about his primate research, widely recognized for its success.

As a result of our visit, we got autographed books and a VIP tour of the zoo. They called the main gate and told them there were some 'officials' from the Olympics who were coming for a zoo tour. They took us behind the scenes and cages. They certainly treated us like we really were officials.

One of the things I told our guide was that we also wanted to the see the cyclorama while we were there.

Well, the tour lasted longer than expected so we were late to the beginning of the cyclorama program. No problem. The guide just called and said to delay the start until some special guests from the Olympics arrived.

Before we left, we took brochures and other materials back to the Olympic Village and shared them with other volunteers.

When I got back to Kearney, I wrote the zoo people a note about how much we appreciated the hospitality. It wasn't long after that, that I got another book about the zoo.

All this happened because Jerry and I were simply looking for a place to have coffee before the gates at the zoo opened.

When Jerry retired from Ventura College, he and Mary moved back to Nebraska. It was home, and their daughter Krista and two grand-daughters lived in Omaha. So, it was a natural transition.

It was a timed filled with major events. Jerry and Mary divorced and Jerry had a series of health issues that included throat, prostate and kidney cancer. You would never have known it. He never wanted to talk about the cancer. He was always most upbeat in everything he did.

Our friends always laughed at pictures of Jerry washing windows on my deck overlooking the golf course in Kearney, stripping wallpaper in a bedroom, painting the steps from the garage into the house or any number of other projects he did. Jerry was the sort of a person who had to be doing something for somebody else all the time.

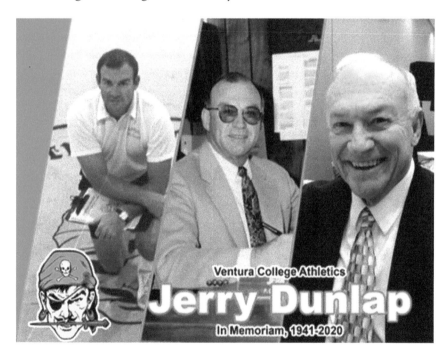

Ventura College Athletics
Jerry Dunlap
In Memoriam, 1941-2020

On September 2, 2020, Jerry and his girlfriend MaryAnn visited Ellen and me in Kearney. Due to COVID 19, it was a short visit. We talked about a winter visit in Arizona and getting together again soon - after he washed the windows on my deck. That was always a given with our friends, Jerry washing windows.

They only stayed a couple of days since Jerry had some doctors' appointments in Omaha when they got back. He actually was sicker than anybody knew, but it never slowed him down.

Two weeks after that visit on September 15, MaryAnn called to say Jerry was struggling with walking and other health issues. Against his wishes, MaryAnn took him to ER in Omaha. He went downhill fast after that. He was down to one kidney, low on magnesium and had a serious bout with Fournier Gangrene.

While Jerry was in the hospital, I talked to MaryAnn or his daughter Krista every day. Only on one occasion was MaryAnn able to hand the phone to Jerry. The only thing I remember was telling him to get well and be good to the nurses. He simply said okay and he would talk to me later.

On the morning of September 30, they moved Jerry to a hospice facility. Mary Ann said her last words to the drivers were to go slow. Jerry loved the beauty of the scenery. They told her they had had many requests, but this was a first.

That evening, Jerry died. His body just wore out.

When they called to tell me with the news, Ellen and I were having dinner with two couples, both friends of Jerry.

I went to my billfold, pulled out the torn dollar bill from those more than 50 years and shared the story of a life of friendship.

The next day, I sent a text picture to Krista asking if she had found Jerry's half since we had talked about it. Later that day she called with the good news, there it was, in his jewelry box – 53 years of memories, lots of laughs and now lots of tears.

Krista said she would get it to me. Didn't want to mail it. Wanted to give it in person. "It's too valuable to mail," she said.

21

Leadership

Leadership, n: difference makers

My relationships with our Alumni Association presidents and board members have both created friendships and enhanced them. Some date to our days together in college and others developed from their service on the alumni board.

Each played a valuable role in the development of the association and its activities.

With their leadership and friendship, the Alumni Association expanded its role with the university.

Among those were an Alumni Advisor program with the Admissions Office that identified alumni in communities of all sizes around the state and Colorado to help with recruiting and alumni events.

With the NU Foundation, the beginning of a Class Agent program was begun.

Other significant accomplishments – a regular alumni magazine, an alumni awards program, a student alumni organization, a scholarship program, a women's mentoring program, reunions and alumni groups around the country and the acquiring of the Alumni House with several renovation projects – were accomplishments of the presidents along with members of the board of directors and our alumni staff.

22

Alumni House

Alumni House, n: a special home

Jodell Payne was president when I became alumni director on a part-time basis in 1978. She was a college friend as was her husband, John, in the 1960s. John was alumni president earlier. John also was my first regular golfing partner at the Kearney Country Club when I came back to Kearney State to teach. As an 18-year member of the University of Nebraska Board of Regents he also was a key player in Kearney State becoming the University of Nebraska at Kearney.

When Jodell was president, the Association was in the process of acquiring a house one block south of campus that became the Alumni House. The home was built in 1907 as a residence for the first president of the college, Dr. A. O. Thomas. It is now on the National Register of Historic Places.

The facility was envisioned as a home for the growing Association. After it was acquired in 1980 the completion of a major renovation in 1987 made that dream complete.

Early in the renovation project, Jodell and I toured the house including a three-car garage that I told her would make a great reception room when completed. It still had an old car stored there and reminded

Jodell of any garage – unfinished, cluttered, musty smelling, oil sills on the floor

Jodell looked at me and said, "Jim, I think you are crazy."

The Alumni House

When the renovation was complete, it did become a special place. Several years later, an addition doubled the size. It has been used for everything from receptions and gatherings to meetings for the campus and community, including a wedding.

Being off-campus and privately owned has always been one of its pluses.

Jodell, along with John, played a key role in its development. When it was first acquired, all the furniture was provided by the Payne family, a gift of their business, Payne-Larson Furniture in Kearney.

23

Playing Santa

Playing Santa, v: giving gifts that make a difference

Judy Henggeler Spohr may best be remembered by her years as the first Golden Girl featured baton twirler of the marching band during her, and my, years as an undergraduate. She went on to an award-winning career as an elementary teacher in East Los Angeles and successful businesswoman in Burbank.

On attending college from Omaha South High School, Judy said, "I wasn't even going to college, I was never really encouraged to do so." But her best friend, Jo Lynn Witham Kuhn, who happened to be the niece of Kearney's football coach Al Zikmund, convinced her to enroll. Judy blossomed.

Her contributions to education, the alumni association, the NU Foundation and the university are significant.

She served as president of the Southern California Alumni Club along with the UNK Alumni Association.

A regular at the Magic Castle in Hollywood, an exclusive club for amateur and professionals along with people who are just fans of magic, Judy befriended a couple, Sam and Doris Fehrenz.

It was there that their friendship blossomed. Later, in declining health, they asked Judy if she could help once a week with groceries. "They didn't have anyone else," she said. Judy helped with that and other things including his estate planning.

Sue Batie, Judy Spohr, Kay Gard, and Al Lybarger all played
an important role in the Southern California Alumni
Association

The estate created two funds at the castle. The rest he wanted to leave to charity.

"I asked him which ones and he said, "You pick them. That's my gift to you," she said. "So, I got to play Santa Claus and write checks."

Those gifts have benefited the Southern California Alumni Association, Omaha South High School and a wide variety of UNK programs – Foster Field improvements, Gold Torch Women's Mentoring program, the Alumni House, her Chi Omega sorority, along with various scholarships.

"I've always believed you should try to make try to make the world a better place," she said. "We all have fantasies about winning the lottery. This generous gift from Sam and Doris has allowed me to do that."

Perhaps the most telling part of Judy's nature is a statement she made at a commencement when she gave greetings to the graduates as alumni president.

"I'm the most proud of three things in my life," she said. "I'm a good mother, a good teacher and a Kearney graduate."

When we were in Southern California for their annual gatherings, a highlight was always a trip to the Magic Castle with the guests from Kearney and Judy. An evening of magic has always been one thing those campus guests always remembered after they got home.

24

Putterheads

Putterheads, n: searchers of golf balls in Kearney Lake

Scott Nelson was Alumni Association president in 1982.

In his home of Lincoln, as president of UNICO Insurance, Scott has been a staple in the community. He also has always been involved in many UNK activities in the area. Our history dated back to his junior high school years in his home of Kearney. I student taught him in the ninth grade. When we would get together in a group often with two other of his classmates – Terry Fairfield, University of Nebraska Foundation president, and Jon Cole, a vice president of Harris Laboratories, I would always start the conversation by saying the we were in junior high together. Of course, Scott would always add, "Sure, he was a student teacher, and I was a student."

For many years, Scott and Jon Cole would return to Kearney for a couple of four-man scramble golf tournaments with Steve Lydiatt and me. It was always a homecoming reunion for those two with their deep connections in the area.

Scott Nelson, me, Steve Lydiatt, Jon Cole

Both remember growing up on the Kearney Country Club and fishing golf balls out of the Kearney Lake. The lake has changed. Not on a bet would either go in it today. I'm not so sure Scott doesn't have more vivid memories of his time as a lifeguard at the country club pool when he was in high school than he does of golf and diving for balls.

25

Memoir

Memoir, n: a place to remember anonymous
stuff

In Tom Smith's memoir, *Name Drop*, he reflected on his college
years in the early 1960s. An active participant in almost every campus
organization, Tom had many stories to recount.

One caught my attention. Here is the way Tom explained it:

Back to my last semester at UNK.

Four of us college graduates to be, when 'refreshing too long'
created '16 Anonymous.' Vanity personified, in flyers we suggested the end of fraternities/sororities, naming professors
whose ties and brains were disgusting and a plethora of other
dumb quips acknowledging the popular Everly Brothers were of
shabby dress and music.

Years later of this 16 Anonymous stuff, an underclassman at
the time was impressed with being a part of this – Jim Rundstrom, the 30-year icon university alumni director. Suzie (Tom's
wife whom he met in college) and I kept our 'Loper' spirit, returning often. So Rundstrom became a very good friend and we
participated in northern Colorado alumni events.

In 1996, he asked if I would like to be on the alumni board. I said, "Wow! Yes."

My third year on the board as president, Jim had established a two-minute presentation at each graduation which I did. Now this guy is a gem never referencing my GPA, my not having any honor society memberships, or as a marginal alumni contributor – but an initiator of the 16 Anonymous.

Years earlier, the 16 Anonymous, thanks to Tom and the other originators, spread it roots and thought a reunion of those crazy times in college would be fun.

Tom Smith and me

Here is the letter to the 30 or so, we could remember and find in 1982.

"Dear XXXX,

"PPSSSSSSSST,

"This is an anonymous invitation.

"Approximately 20 years ago, a group of men at Kearney State (who will remain anonymous) formed a loosely organized society of 16. Shortly thereafter, the society became loosely affiliated with Pi Xi, one of those crazy groups of the 1960s.

"The Pi Xis were best known for their yellow paint cans, pssts, and crooked finger handshakes. Anyway, to many members of both organizations, those days at Kearney State were memorable and fun.

"Now that most of us have had time to clean the yellow paint from under our fingernails and since most of the Pi Xi signs have disappeared from the sidewalks of campus, an anonymous group of former members would like to see some old friends, share some great memories, quaff a beer or two and do whatever might come up."

The letter invited everyone back for Homecoming 1982, a traditional time of alumni gatherings. Many of those on the mailing list were still regulars at events on campus, so getting together was a natural activity.

The reunion was a blast.

26

Golf

Golf, n: a masterful event

Maureen Gaffney Neary was alumni president the year I retired in 2008. At the time she was a Uniserv director for the Nebraska State Education Association. Before working with NSEA, she was an elementary teacher for 26 years with the Grand Island Public Schools. She has since served as a commissioner and board president from District 6 of the Nebraska Department of Education.

As alumni president, Maureen attended a number of alumni events. While traveling on one, our conversation turned to golf, one of my favorite pastimes.

Maureen asked if I had ever been to the Masters Golf Tournament, which I had not. Like most golfers, it had always been a dream to attend. I didn't think much more about what she said until my last board meeting that spring.

Here is Maureen's Masters story that she shared with the board at that meeting.

"When Jim told me he hadn't been to the Masters Tournament, I called my brother Phil, who was a vice president of Club Car golf carts in Augusta, Georgia. He had access to tickets."

Phil knew me from Phi Tau Gamma/Alpha Tau Omega fraternity. Both of us were members, but in different eras. Mine was earlier.

Maureen said, "I told Phil that a day at the Masters would be a terrific retirement gift from the Gaffney family and the Alumni Association."

Phil's reply, "Maureen, we have tickets, but they are spoken for to clients far in advance of the tournament. It is almost impossible. But, let me see what I can do."

Through a series of calls, Phil said he finally had an answer.

"Maureen, how about this?

Instead of just a one-day practice entry, I can do something better, a weekend pass for Lynn and Jim. That really would be special."

Plus, he had a couple of other really special perks.

Phil's mother-in-law had a condo in Augusta and was not going to be there that time of the year. "They can stay there as long as they want. If they fly into Atlanta, we will pick them up and provide them with one of our cars while they are here."

At hearing Maureen's story, I was speechless. Every time I told the story, it was hard to tell without getting choked up.

We decided to drive rather than fly. Did some touring through the horse racing farms of Kentucky and Smokey Mountains in Tennessee, the Jimmy Carter Presidential Library and Museum in Atlanta and Nashville.

The real highlight, though, was walking the grounds of Augusta National for three days. We were the first to arrive in the morning and the last to leave.

Phil and his wife Susan invited us to their house for dinner on the Thursday night we arrived. As a gift to them, we took a case of Nebraska wines from several area wineries. They got a kick out of the Nebraska wines, opening each one for special occasions when they had guests over. When they would do so, Phil and Susan would call me. Part of conversation was how they like the wine.

27

Pen and Ink

Pen and Ink, n: a lost skill in writing

Chuck Lindly was alumni president in 2005. He had a legendary career in education that included superintendent of the Rapid City, South Dakota, schools and professorship in the College of Education at the University of Wyoming.

Following college, Chuck and his wife Marilyn, began their teaching careers in Minden, Nebraska. At an alumni golf outing in Arizona, Chuck was in a foursome with a former student and past alumni president Roger Jones.

Roger said they were standing on a tee box when he said, "Chuck, when you were teaching me social studies in junior high, could you have ever imagined us being together here today?"

Chuck's reply, "Not in my wildest dreams."

One of Chuck's special qualities is we correspond several times a year. Chuck always writes with an ink pen in cursive, usually on UNK cards that we provided him for thank you notes during his term as alumni president. He said it is not easy finding ink in stores anymore. What he does is becoming a lost art.

28

Message Board

Message Board, n: a sign for the times

The university has a message board on U.S. Highway 30. Alumni
presidents Mike McGlade of Omaha and Arlen Osterbuhr of Minden
spearheaded that project to raise $125,000. Before that sign was built,

BEING REPLACED: Alumni Association president-elect Arlen Osterbuhr stands beside the sign that currently promotes campus events along Highway 30. He is holding an architect's rendering of the new Message Center which will replace the trailer sign.

the only messages to passersby was a small message board that could be towed behind a vehicle, parked near an event, and identified with hand-changed letters. It was very efficient although it certainly wasn't attractive.

When driving past the campus, it is always nice to see 'Donated by the UNK Alumni Association' on the sign.

The new message board donated by the Alumni Association

Mike, a former all-American football player and now an adminis-
trator at the University of Nebraska College of Medicine, worked with
retired Loper assistant football coach Terry Renner on his reflections
of more than seven decades of association with athletics.

Terry, who was a college contemporary of mine in the early 1960s,
was an all-conference defensive back. He was assistant football coach at
UNK from 1970 until retiring in 1998.

As Mike said, coach Renner's messages are insightful and "certainly
show a different side of the fella who would tell you as a player, 'If I put
your brain in bird, it would fly backwards,' or 'Do you know why you're
on our third string? It's because we don't have a fourth string' or 'It's
against my better judgment to put you in, but I don't have anyone else.'

Terry wrote 28 devotions reflecting on his journey titled, *It Seems To
Me.* Here are a few of those.

My college football coach, Al Zikmund, had one sign in our
locker room . . . Don't Steal, Don't Lie, and Don't Alibi. As I look
back on my time, I think alibiing (i.e. never my fault) could become a way of life for a lot of us. 'It Seems To Me' never accepting
the responsibility for actions gone wrong can become our crutch.

When I first began coaching, we had a long list of 'training
rules.' I soon came to realize that I could not think of everything.
Life keeps getting more complicated. Gradually, we simplified
our rules to the 'Do Right Rule.' If it's right, okay. If it's not right,
its not okay. As time moved on, we expanded the 'Do Right Rule'
to an action model. 'Be where you are supposed to be, doing what
you're supposed to be doing, when you are supposed to be doing
it.'

When I began applying the 'Do Right Rule' with the action
model to my personal life, my walk of faith became a bit easier.
'It Seems To Me' we are never too old for training rules.

Jumping to the end . . . missing on the present.

During the winter, I have a tendency to look out the window at the snow banks, hear the cold wind, wishing for the warm days of spring and summer. When, in fact, I can still enjoy the present, read a good book, volunteer to make a difference, re-watch a favorite movie, etc., and on a more serious matter, focus on health issues, career decisions and family issues.

Whatever, 'It Seems To Me' we have a tendency to 'jump' to the end. Usually, the end is what frightens us. By staying in the present, enjoying what is good now, spending quality time is important. When we 'jump' to the end, we miss out on so much of the present.

29

Admissions Pro

Admissions Pro, n: expert in recruiting students-athletes

Wayne Samuelson was basketball coach at UNK when I arrived on campus in 1968. I give him credit for turning the program into the success it achieved after he left to become admissions director. When I became director of publications in 1970, recruiting of high school and junior college students was almost a foreign word. We simply provide prospective students or their counselors with basic information about the college and left it at that.

Sam changed that approach.

We worked together on a publication that informally highlighted the campus, a viewbook of strengths and assets of the campus that today is a staple of all colleges and universities. Working with Sam on that publication created a lifelong friendship. We worked together for the university, we traveled together, and we played together. We even refereed a high school basketball game together. Among our favorite 'playing games' were basketball, pitch and the horse races.

Admissions Recruiting Brochure designed by Bill Dunn

Fonner Park, located 45 miles away from Kearney, had life horse races in the spring. For years, Sam organized an outing opening day. It would begin with lunch at his house followed by a meeting at the races. Any activity with Sam always began with food and included snacks.

Sometime before the start of racing season, we would watch 'The Longshot' movie. The1986 comedy featured Tim Conway, Harvey Korman, Jack Weston and Ted Wass, four losers who borrow money from some gangsters to bet on a sure thing at the track. Of course, if they lose, they are faced with an unknown way to repay the loan. It is filled with vintage Tim Conway humor.

Even 30 years later, we watch it again and again.

Sam called our pitch games, often late in the afternoon, 'Scholarship Meetings.' That's the excuse we gave to our office help.

At our noon basketball games, Sam was always in charge of selecting teams. Of course, he always picked the best players and put the other on the opposing team. He would do his best to needle the other players and goad them into shooting more even though they weren't very good.

That was especially true after they made a shot. "You need to be shooting all the time."

Sam was a great admissions person who cared about everyone he came into contact with. One high school counselor told me after Sam had retired that his personal touch was something he really missed. Sam never came to his office without bringing a UNK pen or some other small gift from the admissions office. I always looked forward to his visits, he said.

I was with Sam on one occasion when we got kicked off a college campus. Hiram Scott College in Scottsbluff from 1965 to 1972 announced it was going to close so Sam suggested that we make a trip to Scottsbluff in western Nebraska to discuss with any interested students the opportunity to transfer to Kearney.

We arrived on campus and went to the Registrar's Office to talk to the registrar about setting up a table for students to visit. We hadn't been set up for 15 minutes before the president, Dr. Walter Weese, came by to see what we were doing. Actually, he wasn't interested in what we were doing. He said he wanted us off his campus. He said that when we came on to a college campus, we were to go through proper channels, i.e. the president's office. He said he wanted us to leave.

The registrar, who witnessed the scene, was embarrassed. We started packing up our things while talking to the registrar so it took a few minutes. Before we could finish, Dr. Weese came back and said, "When I told you I wanted you to leave, I meant right now." So, we put our tails between our legs and left. The story became legend around our campus once we got back to Kearney.

30

Art and Soul

**Art and Soul, n: 1. the enthusiasm and
energy gained from art. 2. the deep effect of
art on one person**

As a kid who went to a small catholic high school, I was never exposed to any of the arts. In college, I took an art appreciation class that didn't have much effect except that it did broaden my horizons.

When I came back to Kearney to teach journalism and then direct the program, we were part of the College of Fine Arts and Humanities. One of those departments was art. Several members of that faculty became life-long friends and they have helped me develop a nice collection of works especially from artists that I know. They have also provided me with some good stories.

Jack Karraker was a faculty member when I was a student and when I came back he was the head of the department. In fact, he was on the staff for 45 years and chair of the department for 32, retiring in 2006.

One morning after he retired when we were having coffee, he told a story about shopping at Walmart one afternoon. While checking out, he said encountered a delightful young lady who was working there.

She said, "Professor Karraker, it's nice to see you. You were my art teacher."

Karraker said, "I thought that was very nice. I recognized her but could not remember when I had her in class. So, I asked, 'When was that?'"

Her response, "9:00 this morning."

Keith Lowry, another retired art professor whose landscapes are truly magnificent brought some of his works by my house one afternoon. I bought a couple – one for myself and one for a friend. As he walked around my house, he commented on several of my works, one that especially caught his interest. "That is really nice," he said, "who did it?" I replied, "You did. It's your signature." He just shook his head and said he could hardly remember painting it."

Larry Peterson, who for years has provided our weekly coffee group with rich knowledge of the arts, has played a special role in the art community of all Nebraska. Larry was a key participant in the creation of the Nebraska Art Collection in 1976 and the subsequent beginning of the Museum of Nebraska Art a few years later. When the Nebraska Legislature established the collection on the then Kearney State College campus, it gained state-wide recognition as the third major gallery in Nebraska along with the Joslyn in Omaha and Sheldon in Lincoln.

Larry also began Kearney's Art in the Park in 1971. It is regularly listed among the country's outstanding outdoor art festivals. Among my prized possessions are several Peterson paintings – ones that I have purchased and others that were gifts from him to commemorate special occasions, especially when I retired from the university.

Another special art faculty member was Gary Zaruba. I have always told him I have a Zaruba room in my house with five of his works. Zaruba died at age 74 from complications of cancer and COPD.

We played golf, shared Elks Club activities and other social things. We had a small business together called Design Two. We did newsletters for the businesses and organizations in Kearney. I would do the writing. Z did the design. Before I could afford any art, he gave me a piece from his master's thesis to hang in my house. He also built a fireplace. He was very talented and creative.

Butterfly Wings, 2012 by Gary Zaruba

Dr. Charles Peek, a former faculty member and Episcopalian priest, gave the remarks at his memorial service which was held at the Museum of Nebraska Art, a museum he played a key role in developing.

His comments captured the wonderful qualities of this man and friend.

"As we focus on Z. today, our thoughts probably start at the multiple dimensions of his rich and varied life: he was adept at construction, a maker and repairer of things, an artist in his own right, a curator, a collector – which means a bargainer, buyer, wheedler and cajoler; a teacher and mentor – again, a bargainer, wheedler and cajoler; a husband and lover, a father and a grandparent, a friend and good citizen of his community.

"The message for us this afternoon points to something at the heart of Gary Zaruba's life – the quiet acceptance of the fact that we have very little to do that can affect the creation of life and its ending, that life and death are in God's province, not ours, and that whatever we take to come to some understanding of life and death, a lifetime is not enough to truly grasp the mysteries of God, the mystery that we live with God even when we seem dead in the eyes of this world, that we die in the Lord even when we seem alive, the central mystery that Joseph Campbell tells us is captured in every religion, every mythology, everywhere.

But though the mystery is inexhaustible, many avenues offer ways to glimpse it, apprehend some of it, live into it, let it make sense of our being. We have heard in the scriptures and read how the Middle Easterners of biblical times felt about it. Not far away, the Greeks felt that the ways we approach the great mysteries were to be summed up as Beauty, Truth, and Goodness – each creation or appreciation of something beautiful, each struggle with truth and integrity, each act of loving care leads us into some unity with the divine, make us part of the larger whole around us.

"As Willa Cather put it, 'What was any art but a mold to imprison for a moment the shining elusive element which is life itself - life hurrying past us and running away, too strong to stop, too sweet to lose!'

We are gathered where we might best see the parallels between Beauty, Goodness and Truth – here today the confluence of art and faith, of church and museum. After all, we speak in our churches of the beauty of holiness, and we sometimes term our museums 'temples of beauty.' Some officials of the church are called curates, some officials of the museums are called curators. And yes, I can hear some wit among us saying that both Church and Museum have their collections!

Perhaps that wit is the voice of Gary still speaking with his usual humor here today. Church and Museum, faith and art, goodness and truth – these are just names for avenues we follow in our search for and celebration of life and of life's meaning for us.

Today, they help us celebrate the life of this singular man, the way so many interests and gifts and talents all met in him, how his work and his world of family and friends came together in a sparkling and irreplaceable personality, a person we were blessed to have love us and blessed to have loved.

And this person we have loved is such a presence among us because, as we knew, he was so many persons at once.

He was the man who got plenty tired of dying but never one bit tired of living.

He was the grandfather who loved to support his grandchildren in their activities and sports.

He was the neighbor who so enjoyed living on the lake, finding joy in his neighbors David and Marilyn feeding and watching and tracking the birds who shared their yard and shore.

He was the brother who loved, as he called them, 'the siblings' and their families.

Perhaps you know the Gary Zaruba who enjoyed traveling as long as his health allowed, first with Mary, then with Karen, absorbing the places he cared most for into his own soul, revisiting the southwestern sites.

Perhaps you worked with the Gary Zaruba who knew his Indian art, the art of the American Wet, 19th Century art – knew its pieces, its locations, its artists, was a walking seminar on its beauty and meaning.

Perhaps you enjoyed his laugh, the laughter of his whole face at once, the sense of humor, the good stories, the way he could light up even a dark moment, cheer a weary heart, enrich a gathering.

Like many of you, I knew the artist whose exquisite paintings of our riparian environment, our waters and tree lines, who captured like no other artist the life of this place, the nuances of our fragile existence here on this prairie.

I knew, too, the Z. who was the anchor of the weekly lunches. We would sit as week by week countless friends and former students and colleagues would make their way over to our table, not to speak to any of us, but to greet Gary.

We knew in Gary Zaruba the presence of a gentle, joyful giant of a man. And here we are where his work will live on through the endowment being raised in his name.

Aside from some diminished physical abilities, all those wonderful features that will live with us forever remained alive and well in Gary. Only a couple of weeks ago, we went through our usual routine at lunch.

Someone would get Gary his pudding from the buffet. He'd get a second wind and walk to the entry bench where he'd stop and get his wind again while someone would get the car. Then he'd make it to the car, again catch his breath, and then shut the door.

On this occasion, the next to last of our lunches, an old friend and colleague passed by as Gary collected his breath. Gary got his wind, got into my car, and we headed for his home. When we got there, Z's conversation went like this: wheeze, breath, 'that fellow who passed by us', wheeze, breath, 'there in the restaurant,' wheeze breath, 'he didn't look very well, did he?'

Gary's great soul was merry to the end.

Much of our grief is assuaged by the knowledge that what we see is really just wrappings, that the reality of us lives on with God. We know Gary to be now at peace in the healing presence of the love that game him being. We know we will carry him always in our hearts.

Zaruba was a living example of the goal of living as it was described by the anthropologist Ashley Montague: to die as old as possible still as young as we can be. May he rest in the piece his painting captured. May he always know God's love and ours.

31

Sunny Disposition

Sunny Disposition, n: friendships sustained through winter retirement in Arizona

Scott Robinson and I first met when we were freshmen teammates on the basketball team in college. That was the extent of our college athletic experience. As we soon realized, neither was good enough to make it a second year. We were in different fraternities but stayed close socially. I have awarded Scott a prized university record. He took classes every semester for seven consecutive years before he graduated.

He and his wife, whom he met in college, Bonita (Mitch) Buckhammer, shared a long teaching career in Manning, Iowa. Scott always said she had two qualities that attracted him to her, she had a job and a car. Mitch would respond that the thing she liked best about Scott was his friends. They were married for 50 years before we lost both of them within a two-year period in 2018 and 2019.

They were our closest friends in Arizona where they spent six months away from the Iowa winters.

Scott was never without a quip.

A couple of former students were visiting them in Arizona where they spend the winter. One was rather large. Scott made the comment to her one day. "Julie, I think the pockets on your jeans have gotten smaller since last year."

I fell and broke two ribs one evening coming out of the Elks Club in Sun City, Arizona, after an evening of fun with Scott and Mitch. Of course, I blamed Scott. But they did take me to the emergency room two days later at 10:30 pm when I called and told them I hurt so bad I couldn't get in bed. I know they would do anything I needed.

32

Honored Service

Honored Service, n: recognition for work honoring others

Through my years as a faculty member and alumni director I was fortunate to work with a number of people in the athletic department. Many of those became special friends.

Two, John McBride and Dick Beechner, surprised me with an announcement that, unknown to me, the Hall of Fame committee had voted to induct me in the Meritorious Service category.

They both were appreciative of my involvement in starting the Hall of Fame and serving as selection committee chair since its1980 inception along with developing Hall criteria.

McBride said it was one the last things he wanted to do while AD. Dick Beechner and John McBride both served on the Hall of Fame committee so I asked Dick to introduce me at the Homecoming banquet when the inductions took place.

Dick has been a consummate volunteer for every community project and has been a key individual in several state athletic hall of fames – golf and the Nebraska High School Hall of Fame. A Lincoln native, he knows everyone by virtue of his coaching football at UNL, Washington State, Missouri and Hiram Scott College in Scottsbluff. After he stepped down as UNK athletic director, he continued to coach the university golf team.

Larry Feather, Roger Jones, Larry Edwards, UNK Athletic
Director John McBride, Denny Renter, Dave Jones, me

His local, regional and state recognitions are legendary as is his sense of humor.

When I had the opportunity to respond at the Hall of Fame banquet, I thanked him for his introduction and said he nearly gave me a chance to be a college golf coach.

One spring, he asked me to take the team to a tournament in Gothenburg, sixty miles away since he could not go.

I said, "Dick, does that mean I'm the coach?" His reply was, "No, you are the van driver."

"Well, then, what do you want me to do?" I asked.

He said, "Get the van first thing in the morning, pick the boys up at the Health and Sports Center at 8:00. When you get to Gothenburg, give them golf balls.

"Then check on them while they are playing to see if they need water or a drink. Take them lunch. Record their scores when they are done. When you get back to Kearney, take them to USA Steak Buffet for dinner.

"Repeat the same routine on day two."

I said, "Dick, what else does a golf coach do?"

My induction speech in that 2013 event also paid tribute to Don Briggs, who was an institution at Kearney.

It went something like this:

One of the people we are missing this year is long-time professor and sports information director Don Briggs who passed away last winter. He played such an important role in this campus and everything associated with it, especially the Hall of Fame.

One of Mr. B's endearing qualities was that he timed every Homecoming acceptance speech. So, Mr. B, I know you have your watch ready for what I have to say.

UNK athletics has provided me, and my family, with a lifetime of enjoyment. Those athletic events have been an important part of my life since I was a student in the early 1960s and even more so after I came back on the staff in 1968. At the Rundstrom house as my kids would tell you, blue and gold were always our favorite colors – and our only colors.

Our lives revolved around activities on the campus and, especially, any sporting event. Todd reminded me of many of his favorite memories – trips to Kansas City for the NAIA basketball tournament and climbing to the top of the old press box at Kearney's Foster Field when I filmed football games. That press box, by the way, certainly was nothing like we have today. Even the slightest wind made it sway.

Tracy, always my bookworm, said we went to so many events that she took a book to read. She also remembered her strategy of going to the concession stand exactly three minutes before halftime to beat the crowd.

When I asked Tammy, she remembers me dragging her to every sporting event there was – no matter what the sport. And often dressing as a UNK cheerleader for Halloween. The Alumni Association sponsored the Spirit Squad for a number of years and the girls would go through the old uniforms which were stored in the attic of the Alumni House.

All in all, it was, and still is, great family entertainment. As a family, we reveled in the athletic teams' successes and we suffered in the defeats.

But the most important part of the years of my association with athletics has been the relationships that developed and the lifelong friends who grew out of those connections. Those friendships have enriched my life way beyond my ability to express it.

I am honored to be included among those who are in the Athletic Hall of Fame especially when my role has been nothing more than to vicariously share in the accomplishments of others. Those Hall of Fame members who have been inducted the past 34 years represent thousands of other athletes, coaches and contributors to the program whose dedication created a legacy to this university.

The Hall of Fame is a permanent reminder of those individual achievements. But, equally important, is that those individuals are tied to teammates and others who, although may not be in the Hall of Fame, played important roles that made it possible for others to achieve that goal.

To have my family and friends here tonight – who have come from places like Texas, California, Oregon, Colorado, Missouri, Kansas an many other places – makes this a very special event. I can't imagine why I should be included in the Hall of Fame. But I will be forever grateful for everyone who played a role in making it possible.

33

Coaching Lessons

Coaching Lessons, n: advice and mentorship from a trusted coach

Other than my parents, Don Briggs has had more of an influence in my career than anyone else. He had a hand in both jobs I have had.

I took my first journalism class from Mr. B, as we called him, when I was a sophomore in college. For years, I kept those notes. As I said at a fraternity event when I spoke about his influence on many of us in that room, the fact that I had notes was probably a big surprise to him. He probably couldn't remember my coming to class. I did attend but not always on a regular basis.

Curiosity. Eye for precise detail. Integrity. Attention to brevity. Accuracy. Hard work. Those were things he believed in. They were how he lived his life.

Mr. B. often brought quirky examples of stories and humorous misprints he collected from a variety of newspapers.I used one of his handouts for years primarily because it taught, in a very simple way, how important clear writing is. These were some of those examples.

Harry Mahan has bought a cow and is now supplying his neighbors with milk and eggs.

Miss Perkins will have a baby at the meeting so that she can illustrate the points to look for.

As the reverend Bragg performed the ceremony, the bride donned a floor-length gown of white lace.

For their breakfast, the newly-married couple had a cup of coffee and a roll in bed.

Communication by road, air and by wife was completely disrupted by the storm.

The General and his wife have no children. His hobby is golf.

One of the most considerate things noted in a long time was last week when Silas Hawkins buried his wife, ill for some time.

Several excuses for students illustrate the same need for accuracy.

Chris has acre in his side.

Ralph as absent yesterday because of sour trout.

Please excuse Wayne from being absent yesterday, because he had the fuel

Please excuse Roland from P.E. for a few days. Yesterday he fell out of a tree and misplaced his hip.

Please excuse John for being absent Jan. 28, 29, 30, 31, 32, 33.

Mary could not go to school because she had very close veins.

Please excuse Gloria. She has been sick and under the doctor.

Sometimes you don't realize how stupid some of the things you write really are. Don Briggs taught me that.

His influence on the fraternity was legendary. It was originally Phi Tau Gamma as a local fraternity and later affiliated with Alpha Tau Omega in the mid-1960s when the Greek organizations on campus developed national affiliations.

When Phi Tau Gamma purchased a fraternity house in 1961, it would not have happened if Don had not been willing to live there as a supervisor or 'House Mother.' In the college yearbook, there is a great picture of a dozen pledges with our beanies on shoveling snow at the fraternity house in the height of the storm. Right in the middle giving directions is Don.

Don Briggs and me

On Saturday mornings he was always at the fraternity house with reminders, in his own gentle way, that 'by damn we had better get up and get the place cleaned.'

Don was responsible for the only two jobs I ever had.

When I was a senior in college, he personally lined up an interview with the superintendent of schools in Sidney. Made me go to the interview, too. I ended up teaching there and met my wife while in Sidney.

When I was in graduate school at Kansas State four years later, thanks in large part to a letter of recommendation from Don, I got a call from him during the spring semester. And, it wasn't easy to find me since it was before cell phones.

He finally got a hold of me at Lynn's Kappa Alpha Theta sorority house at UNL when one of her sorority sisters told her that some guy from Kearney was looking for me. His name was on the phone log.

I called him and our conversation went something like this:

Briggs: Well, how's school? When are you going to graduate?

Me: School is good. I am going to graduate this summer.

Briggs (Knowing my past academic record, said): Are you sure you'll graduate?

Me: It certainly looks like I'll make it.

Briggs: Well then, what are you going to do after that?

Me: I don't know. I am getting married in June. But I don't have a job.

Briggs: Well, if you want a job, you need to get down here to Kearney and talk to Harry Hoffman (Dr. Hoffman was dean of the college of fine arts and humanities). We have a journalism teaching job that includes advising the college yearbook and you might be able to do the job. I'll talk to Harry if you are interested.

Of course, I was. To return to your college to teach at age 26, was an impossible dream. Especially with the academic record I had at Kearney.

I have shared this story often, too. More than any other, it illustrates my academic career as an undergraduate.

When I arrived on campus that fall of 1968 to begin teaching, the first faculty meeting was with the English Department since journalism was not an entity in itself but part of English.

Like many, I wondered if any of my former teachers would remember me. Walking up the stairs of the Administration Building, I encountered Miss Dorothy Klein, who I had for a couple of classes. She looked at me, smiled as she recognized me. I was thrilled. Then, Miss Klein said, "Jim Rundstrom, nice to see you. Are you coming back to finish your degree?"

I am sure I aged her years when I told her I was going to begin teaching Journalism.

At that time in 1968, Mr. B served in a variety of capacities on campus. He was Mr. Everything at Kearney State. He had sponsored student government, was sports information director, handled any alumni activities, prepared all college publications, did all of his own printing of college publications in the college print shop.

Now there are a dozen or so people doing those jobs.

Oh, yes, he also taught journalism and English.

A pioneer in the collegiate sports information field, Briggs was deeply involved in NAIA activities. For more than 20 years, he was 'Mr. NAIA' for serving as the press room coordinator for the NAIA track and field championships and for the NAIA national basketball tournament in Kansas City. He was inducted into the NAIA Hall of Fame for meritorious service in 1971 and twice received the NAIA Award of Merit. In 1980 he was named the NAIA Sports Information Director of the Year.

His fraternity contributions are also legendary. He was ATO National Adviser of the Year and received the ATO Lifetime Achievement Award.

Among the many awards he received were the UNK Distinguished Alumni Award, the Kearney Hub Freedom Award for Service and induction into the UNK Athletic Hall of Fame for his lifetime of service.

Briggs once said that the best part of his years at Kearney was his association with students. "My door was always open every day of the week, evenings and weekends. People were always stopping by to give me a hard time, or vice versa."

When I got involved with the Alumni Association, the one thing I was smart enough to know that the most valuable resource I had was Don Briggs. He knew everyone. Every day I stopped by his office I learned a little more. I can never remember a time when I stopped that he did not have a clipping about some alumnus from the scads of newspapers he read every day.

Don Briggs certainly was Kearney State. A life-long bachelor, the college was his life. He was always there.

Literally.

As a student, Barry Sherman said he remembers coming home to Stout Hall late one night and Don's light was on in his office in the Student Union. It was not uncommon. He practically lived there.

Industrial arts professor Maynard Envick said he often came back at night to check on projects, Don was at his other home on campus, the Print Shop, where he was continually working on some publication.

For me, "I never thought of looking for him any place other that his office or the print shop. If he wasn't there, I would begin to worry about him."

As sports information director, Don did everything at sporting games. He announced, he helped referees officiate with his suggestions on the PA system, he kept stats, he took pictures, and he even handled crowd control.

He endeared himself to all Kearney State basketball fans when he told rival Hastings College coach Lynn 'Doc' Farrell to sit down during a game. Typically, fans chanted that during the game, but Don got caught up and said "Sit down, coach," over the public address system. It took post-game apology, letters to the Hastings president and coach Farrell, and time before things calmed down.

The story is legend and probably illustrates more than anything else, Don Briggs' passion for Kearney.

I filmed for the football team for nine years. On trips, Don would often drive his own car whether it was to LaCrosse, Wisconsin; Pittsburg, Kansas; or Billings, Montana.

One weekend we played in Pittsburg, 600 miles away. Don and I left with three freshmen at 5:30 am Saturday morning, saw the sun come up south of Minden, played the game at night in Pittsburg, drove home and saw the sun come up about the same place Sunday morning.

He drove the entire way.

By Sunday afternoon Don was in his office compiling NAIA District 11 statistics which he did every Sunday for many years.

In addition to being a model around campus, Don could have been a model for Jeff McNelly's comic strip SHOE.

Shoe

Shoe Comic Strip

Whether it's the drill sergeant barking orders to the maggots at summer camp like fraternity pledges, the 'perfessor' who can't find his desk for all the things piled on it or the one of the coaches talking to his little quarterback, the comic strip resonated with me.

This conversation in particular always reminded me of Don.

Our athletes at Kearney are testaments about how true that really is.

I wrote in his death notice in the alumni magazine that for more than 60 years, this place was his life.

34

Southern Hospitality

Southern Hospitality, n: a deep friendship with Texans

When I lived in Sidney from 1964 to 1967, Mike Hardy was one of the few people my age who lived there. After he had returned from Vietnam, he moved to Sidney where his dad and step-mother had relocated from east Texas. His accent was definitely not Nebraska. I always said that he was the only person I knew who pronounced the word 'shit in two syllables - 'She-it.

He met a Sidney girl, Barb Christ, and eventually returned to Longview, Texas. Barb and Lynn were friends. The Christ family and my in-laws were social friends, as were each of their parents. Three generations. Barb tells the story of living with the Robinson family for several weeks when a family medical situation posed a problem. The girls' friendship ran deep.

Lynn and I were married June 8, 1968. Mike and Barb June 30, 1968. We were all part of each others' weddings.

In Texas, they are family to my daughters Tracy and Tammy. Barb hosted bridal showers for both girls and have shared in their Texas activities.

When Tracy was a college student at TCU, she often spent vacation times at the Hardy house in Longview when it was not possible to come back to Nebraska for things like Thanksgiving and Easter. Now they attend the grandkids school events and continue to be a part of their lives.

Mike and Barb were in my hospital room when coach Kropp and Larry arrived to take me back to Nebraska. They, and the nurses were the ones with huge smiles when they walked in. "These are the two guys who don't have cell phones?" they asked.

Mike and Barb Hardy

Mike spent many years as manager of an Edwin Watts' Golf Shop. Most of my golf supplies were courtesy of Mike. In my hospital room I had a new pair of Adidas golf shoes I had just gotten from Mike the day before I suffered the leg issue. Jokingly, I asked Mike if I could return the right shoe since I had doubts I would need it for a long time. I would keep the left shoe since that was my good leg.

No deal, he said. I had to keep both.

As it worked out, I never did wear those shoes. After four years, I gave them to Roger Jones. Well, actually I traded them for a bottle of

Kettel One vodka. It certainly was a good deal for me. And for Roger, too.

Barb and my daughters Tracy and Tammy celebrate their mother Lynn's birthday with lunch every year since her death.

35

Trippers

Trippers, n: travel experiences

Barry Sherman and I traveled together to alumni events when he was director of development for the Kearney State Foundation. On one of our trips to Southern California, he encountered an unusual event that even had local police shaking their heads.

Faculty member Miriam Drake and Earl Rademacher were special guests of the Southern California group in 1982.

Earl arrived late on a Friday night at LAX. Barry and I picked him up and drove to our hotel, the Disneyland Apollo Inn. Barry had a duffel bag that he sat by the car while going with Earl to register.

When Barry came back, the bag was gone. After searching until nearly midnight, Barry called the police. They arrived, got Barry's statement that included the contents of the bag. The police left and Barry went outside the motel room trying to figure out what happened.

That's when he saw a motorcycle slowly drive through the parking lot. The driver was wearing Barry's jacket and his running shoes. Barry ran downstairs into the street and followed the motorcycle into an adjacent motel parking lot.

Barry got the license number of the motorcycle and called the police. The police traced the guy down to an apartment a mile away, arrested him and found everything. The guy was even wearing Barry's socks. Barry told the police the guy could keep the socks.

Barry was able to identify things like his Nike running shoes and even a book of matches in the pocket of his jacket. The police and Barry also returned to his apartment where, going through the trash, they found Barry's return flight airplane tickets and his keys.

It was 3:00 am when he got back. This, mind you, was in Anaheim, California.

Barry was involved in another memorable incident in our alumni adventures.

This time in Phoenix, Arizona, in the spring of 1984.

We had flown in on a Sunday running for a gathering at the home of alums Larry and Del Ludden who lived on the Biltmore Golf Course. The event was scheduled for noon.

College president William Nester, his wife Mary Jane, Barry and I checked into our hotel to change before going to the Ludden house. We had just arrived from our Southern California event which was the night before.

The only problem was that I had a room, the president for some reason didn't. The receptionist at the desk had no reservation for him and no record of his office making one. He was not the type of person to take that message well.

And, they were booked full for the evening.

I offered my room to the Nesters, but they declined. They said they would use my room to change and find a place later which was fine. Changing clothes took time so I'm nervous, thinking we were running late for the brunch. Barry and I waited outside checking our watches. And we waited.

Eventually, the Nesters arrived with their luggage which they put in the back of the hatchback I had rented. As the president was backing away from the car, I, inadvertently, slammed the hatchback on his head. It wasn't too hard, but it did stun him. I felt terrible but couldn't do anything about it but apologize. Which I did. Dr. Nester was never known for having a sense of humor and this certainly wasn't funny at the time, so not much was said on the 20-minute ride to the Ludden house. Actually, after my apology, nothing was said.

Word travels fast. When we got back to the campus, the story had already begun making the rounds on campus.

"JR slammed Nester's head in the trunk of his car in Arizona."

Depending on one's opinion of the president, I was either the most popular person on campus for what I did. Or, for some, I was not at a high level of esteem since, according to them, I didn't hit him hard enough. Long after Dr. Nester retired and moved back to Cincinnati, the episode was repeated over drinks at cocktail parties.

Barry and I both survived.

However, Barry left the foundation later that spring. But he always watched his head when traveling with me.

36

Making a Mark

Making a Mark, v: leaving a branded legacy

Another favorite UNK chancellor event was the statewide introduction of our new chancellor Gladys Styles Johnston in 1992.

Dr. Johnston was a black woman who came to UNK from Chicago. She had never been to western Nebraska, a part of the state that the university served regionally. We organized a plane trip using the University of Nebraska Foundation plane that included several stops including Lodgepole.

Lodgepole, a village of about 400, didn't have an airport but had a number of alumni and great supporters including the banker, E.K. Yanney, and a wheat farmer, Dale Kastens, who was also president of the UNK Alumni Association.

Both were community leaders. The Lodgepole baseball field is named Kastens Field for the volunteer work that both Dale and his wife, Jeanine, did.

When Dale was alumni president, I always introduced him as a true friend of the university. This event for the chancellor was a perfect example.

However, I always added another bit of information.

After graduating from junior college in Scottsbluff, I said, Dale set a UNK record of graduating in three terms – Eisenhower, Kennedy and Johnson. Actually, that was true. He started when Eisenhower was president in 1959 and graduated when Johnson was president in 1964.

When the chancellor's plane landed the plane in Chappell, a community of about 1,500 eight miles east of Lodgepole, I'm sure it was her first time landing on such a small runway with no terminal. When we landed, our ground transportation, a small Lodgepole school bus drove right next to the plane.

The chancellor's eyes lit up as she shook her head at such a scene. We all boarded the school bus for the quick trip to Lodgepole.

UNK Chancellor Gladys Styles-Johnston
and me

Our first stop was a blacksmith shop, something they were sure the chancellor had never seen. The people wanted her to get a flavor of western small-town Nebraska and its hospitality.

The blacksmith welcomed the chancellor. "You're not from around here, are you?" he asked. She replied that she had never been to western Nebraska.

He was showing her around the shop when she asked him what those things on the wall were. They were branding irons that he had forged.

He looked at her and said, "You really aren't from around here, are you?"

Then he explained the branding process.

Following that tour, we headed to a reception at the Lodgepole State Bank. It was a huge event for this community to have the chancellor of the university attend a reception. She endeared herself to those there when she repeated the blacksmith story. She then said the only thing she needed to make the stop complete was a cowboy hat like the one someone who was in attendance was wearing.

A cowboy hat for her arrived at her office the next week.

37

Kerry-smatic

Kerry-smatic, adj: unique and endearing way people are drawn to Kerry Kimple

Every morning for most of my career at the university, I started with coffee and a roll first at Sehnert's Bakery in downtown Kearney then at Daylight Donut.

Another regular was Kerry Kimple, a computer technology salesman who worked for a company that sold a variety of assessment programs and athletic scouting programs.

Kerry was a huge sports enthusiast. He played freshman basketball at Kearney and officiated high school and junior college basketball for years.

In 1990, NFL commentator John Madden was traveling through Nebraska in his Madden Cruiser when he stopped at Grandpa's Steakhouse, a popular restaurant near where the Kimple family lived. The Madden Cruiser was an iconic symbol of his travel priorities since he didn't fly.

As Madden tells the story in a November 26, 1990, issue of *Sports Illustrated* about his travels across the country, he said, "While we were eating, the Kerry Kimple clan of Kearney collected near the bus, waiting outside." When Madden went outside, the family with son Travis, age 10, daughter, Lindsy, age 7, and his Kerry's wife, Shari, were there to meet him.

The Kimples got a tour of the bus and plenty of pictures. In telling the story to others, Kerry said, "Kearney loves John Madden. He's a common sense, say-what-he-thinks guy."

"I like Kearney, and let me tell you, the barbecue in this town is great." — John Madden

BIG MAN BACK IN TOWN

Hub photo by Todd Gottula

A photo, upper left, of legendary NFL coach and broadcaster John Madden signing a football at Grandpa's Steakhouse for Lindsy and Travis Kimple of Kearney appeared in Sports Illustrated in 1990. Madden stopped in Kearney Friday and Lindsy, now a senior at Kearney High School, met him again.

Monday Night Football's John Madden lunches at Kearney BBQ restaurant, renews acquaintance from 1990

PERSONAL FILE

Name: John Madden
Age: 66
Residence: Pleasanton, Calif.
Family: Wife, Virginia; two sons
Career Highlights: Before joining the broadcasting ranks, Madden had an outstanding career as head coach of the NFL's Oakland Raiders from 1969-1978. He guided the Raiders to an over-all record of 103-32-7, leading the team to seven AFC Western Division titles and a victory over the Minnesota Vikings in Super Bowl XI. Madden's winning percentage (.750) is the best of any head coach in NFL history. After 21 seasons as an NFL analyst for CBS and FOX, Madden joined ABC's Monday Night Football this season.

By TODD GOTTULA
Hub Staff Writer

© Copyright 2002 Kearney Hub Publishing Co.

KEARNEY — Kerry Kimple of Kearney was smiling ear to ear Friday after-noon, and his 16-year-old daughter, Lindsy, was almost speechless. And John Madden? Well, he was just typical John Madden.

"I like Kearney, and let me tell you, the barbecue in this town is great. I've always liked Nebraska, and today has been a beautiful day to be on the road," said the legendary NFL broadcaster, who is in his first season as analyst for ABC's Monday Night Football. "Great fall weather means great football, and you know all about that here in Nebraska, right?"

WHILE TRAVELING from Seattle to Pittsburgh for Monday's game between the Steelers and Indianapolis, Madden and his traveling party of three stopped at Kearney's Skeeter Barnes restaurant near Interstate 80 to grab lunch.

Madden, 65, and the Madden Cruiser slipped into town about 2:30 p.m., and he left an hour later after feasting on chicken wings, a pulled chicken sandwich, loaded baked potato and iced tea. "When he walked in the door, we had to look twice. We were just

The alternative to flying is the Madden Cruiser.

See ♦ BIG MAN, page 7A

Great story.

It was a perfect way to describe the popular announcer and former NFL coach,

End of story.

Nope.

Twelve years later, in 2002, the bus was on its way through Kearney again on a fall Friday night, when they stopped at a barbeque diner, Skeeter Barnes, across the street from Grandpa's Steakhouse.

Kerry happened to be driving home about that time when he spotted the bus. He went in and asked Madden if he would autograph the pictures Kerry had taken 12 years earlier.

"If you are going to be around here awhile, I'll go get them." Kerry said.

Daughter Lindsy, a senior in high school, was home getting ready for Homecoming football that night where she was a candidate for queen. By then, Travis was 22 and a senior in college at UNK.

Lindsy went back to the restaurant with her dad, got the pictures signed and had a chance to visit with Madden. "She was 4-years-old when I met her the first time, now she's all grown up," he said.

Both, the 1990 picture and the 2002 picture were featured in *Sports Illustrated* in the Faces in the Crowd section.

Madden said, "You think how big this country is and all the things that can happen and not happen to you. This proves it is a small world.

As a computer software salesman, Kerry always had stories of his meetings with clients and his travels. One morning on a trip to Omaha, he had a flat tire. Not normally a big problem.

He got out of his car, looked in the trunk. No spare.

"So, I called AAA road assistance," he said. "They arrived much sooner than I expected. So, I'm thinking, this guy will deserve a nice tip."

I suggested he tow me to the nearest tire shop where I could get a new tire. No problem. However, AAA only paid for the first 10 miles. The rest was my responsibility. That amounted to $220. Then, I had to buy a new tire. Another $90. So, my bill was $300, before the tip.

Then the tow truck driver said. "You know you have a spare tire. It's just not in the trunk in this car." Kerry said he thought, Thanks a lot.

There went his tip.

Traveling around the state has provided Kerry with a wealth of stories.

One afternoon in 2002, he was in Omaha and met a college friend Jeff Kerr at Omaha Benson High School where he taught. Jeff asked Kerry if he had ever met their football coach, Lonnie Tapp.

Kerry had not, so Jeff said, "He's a great guy and character. Let's run down to his office. Coach, meet Kerry Kimple" Kerr said. They visited for a few minutes.

School had just gotten out and coach Tapp was headed out to football practice.

He also noticed the obvious, Kerry was bald. Tapp told Kerry he reminded him of Miami University coach Larry Corker, who was head coach of the Hurricanes from 2001 to 2006.

"Do you want to come out and watch practice?" he asked.

'Sure," Kerry said.

On the way out, coach Tapp said, "I've got a kid I want you to meet." He called over Tierre Green.

"Tierre," he said," this is Miami University football coach Larry Coker. He came all the way from Miami to watch you practice. 'Coach Coker, do you have anything you want to say to Tierre?"

Kerry recalls, "I didn't see that coming, but was able to say, 'Tierre, do you want to play college football?'"

Tierre's response was, "Yes sir. I do."

"Tierre, do you practice hard all the time?"

His answer was another polite, "Yes, sir."

Again.

"That's great," Kerry said. "Because you play like you practice."

"Now get out there and work hard," Kerry said.

"Yes, sir," Tierre replied.

Kerry said he stayed awhile and watched some practice. Teirre worked really hard. Coach Tapp later said it was the hardest he had seen Tierre practice.

Tierre was a very good player who went on to Nebraska where he was a defensive back for four years. He started every game as a safety his junior and senior year, 2006 and 2007.

He never did know that coach Larry Coker was never at his practice.

Kerry has always been quick with a story. Assistant director of the Alumni Association, Kristin Howard, shared a story about Kerry one morning in 2002 shortly after Doug Kristensen was named chancellor at UNK, Kerry stopped by my office. Kerry and the chancellor were high school classmates in Minden.

Kristin, whose office was upstairs from mine in the Alumni House, recalls that she came down stairs to see me. I was not in my office, but Kerry was there. "I introduced myself," she said.

Kerry then said, "Kristin, nice to meet you. I'm Doug Kristensen, your new chancellor."

"I believed him," she said. Kerry looked nothing like the chancellor, but was quick thinking so knew a couple of stories to tell her.

Kristin said she never did know that Kerry wasn't the chancellor until she met him.

He was that convincing.

38

Student Development

Student Development, n. encounters with lifetime student friends

As director of the Journalism Program for nearly 20 years, I had unlimited opportunities for encounters with students. My office was a place to talk about class schedules, career opportunities, graduation requirements and a variety of other things. Many of those visits were about personal issues.

Some had stories that I can recall easily and some are from later encounters that they hadn't shared with me when they were students.

Nancy Divis

Nancy Divis was a college senior when I took the job as yearbook advisor. She was the first student I met during my interview since she was going to be the yearbook editor the next year. She later told me she wasn't happy when I was hired since her connection to the yearbook was with the professor who left, one that she really liked. We became lifelong friends and still stay in touch more than 50 years later sharing personal and professional stories.

Stephanie Hueftle Vogel

When I became full-time alumni director in 1989, I hired one person to go with me. Stephanie was a work-study in the Journalism department who was getting ready to graduate – in three years.

She was in my office that spring talking about a position in television she had interviewed for. After hearing about that offer, I asked her if she had any interest in going with me as assistant director. I explained to her that it would be just us two so our jobs were everything from being secretary to custodian. She said yes!

Lynn, me, Stephanie Hueftle Vogel, Rita Jones, Roger Jones

It was an important day. One of the most significant contributions was her key role in beginning a women's mentoring program she named The Gold Torch Society.

That program, which was begun in 2000, brought together 25 alumni and 25 students for a fall weekend of events on campus to explore career opportunities and issues. Each alumnus is partnered with an upperclass student who was chosen from an application process.

Through the years many of the alumni mentors and their student mentees have developed long-time relationships.

Another value of the program was the opportunity to bring successful women graduates back to campus. Gold Torch is still a popular Alumni Association program after 20 years.

Celann LaGreca

As a freshman, Celann LaGreca came into my office one spring day to tell me that she couldn't type, but she knew it was a required skill she needed since her goal was to have a career in public relations. That summer Celann and her dad, a career educator, made a trip to Kearney to see what could be done.

I had her enroll in a business department typing class that fall.

As Celann likes to tell the story in gatherings, she really struggled with the class and ended up getting a B grade. It was her only B in college. Oh, yes, she also reminds everyone that I had failed to tell her that she could have taken the class pass/fail.

My smiling response has always been that it really affected her career. She went on to have an extremely successful public relations career as a vice president of Blue Cross of Nebraska. She has served on numerous boards including the Nebraska State College Board of Trustees.

She also received a Distinguished Alumni Award from the Alumni Association. After an early retirement from Blue Cross, Celann started LaGreca Group, a firm that specializes in strategy, marketing and public relations consulting.

Dianne Gabrukiewicz Bystrom

When Dianne Gabrukiewicz Bystrom was a junior in college, she was involved in everything on campus – Alpha Phi sorority and a cheerleader since her freshman year were among those. More than anything else, she was a terrific student. One spring day, I called her into my office for a visit. "Dianne, you should apply to be editor of the Antelope student newspaper next year. It is exactly the type of experience your college academic career needs. But, you are going to have to give up your favorite activity - cheerleading."

It wasn't what she wanted to hear, but she did it.

When fall rolled around, she prepared to publish her first issue when classes began. Early in that process, Dianne came into my office in tears. "JR, I don't know what to do. I don't have enough stories to fill the first issue. You said I could do it and you would help me. What are WE going to do?"

I had taught a feature writing class the previous spring and one of the assignments was to write a feature story about a person or something on campus – one that would be suitable for publication. When the tears dried, we went through those stories that were still appropriate for use. After the first couple of issues, things became easier.

Dianne graduated magna cum laude and had a great career in public relations and higher education.

She began as a reporter at a weekly newspaper and retired from Iowa State University where she was director of the Carrie Chapman Catt Center for Women in Politics for 22 years.

Along the way, she was co-author or co-editor of 21 books.

When Dianne received her Ph.D. from the University of Oklahoma, her husband, Keith, asked me, along with numerous others, to send a note of congratulations.

I included the newspaper editor episodes but also a story about Dianne house sitting for us one summer when we were on a family vacation. It wasn't a disaster, but Dianne left a hot pan on a kitchen counter that left a burnt ring. She was devastated.

Of course, sarcastic and sympathetic me, I told the story in my congratulation letter. Since we had just moved, I said one of the reasons we bought a different house was because we would have had to renovate the kitchen and it was cheaper to buy a new house.

Her career has been filled with awards from women's groups, Iowa State University and a Distinguished Alumni Award from UNK.

Mike Darbro

Years after graduating, Mike Darbro shared a story I had forgotten. Early in his senior year, he came into my office and surprised me by saying he wasn't going to be able to graduate. He said he needed a science class to fulfill a general studies requirement and was certain there was no way he could pass one. Absolutely, no way.

As Mike tells the story, I said, "Let me make a call to Dr. Laddie Bicak." He was the chair of the Biology Department. I told Laddie the situation, sent Mike over to see him. Dr. Bicak, one of the really helpful and good guys on the staff, asked Mike what he needed. Mike said he just had to pass one science class. Dr. Bick told Mike to enroll in Biology 100, come to class, take the tests and he would take care of it. Mike said when he got a 'D' for a grade, he may have been the happiest guy on campus. He graduated!

Tammy Moerer

Tammy Moerer arrived at Kearney State, a farm girl from Johnson, Nebraska, in the mid-1970s. She was bright, pretty and most outgoing. She was an ideal college student except, like lots of others, she wasn't sure what she wanted to do. But she did want to major in public relations, a perfect choice.

One of her talents, which I learned later, was that she was a state champion hog caller. She learned that growing up on her family farm.

That was a talent that served her well from a college coed point of view. When Tammy and her friends made the usual Thursday night stop at a college water hole, The Buffalo Chips, her friends and college bar tenders tried to coax her into giving the hog call. Her response, "only for a pitcher of beer. A free couple of beers took care of us for the night," she said.

We still get together in Cave Creek, Arizona, during our winter stay there at a local spot named The Buffalo Chip. How appropriate.

Tammy was chosen Nebraska hog queen, and made the rounds for the hog producers association. As a junior, she was chosen National

Hog Queen. That meant missing a lot of school performing duties at national events.

Tammy came into my office after she was chosen and said she was going to take a semester off since she wouldn't have time for classes. I talked her out of it by working out a schedule that included credit for internship, public relations and feature writing. It turned out well since it kept her on schedule to graduate.

Tammy often tells the story of coming into my office with a gift after our third child was born in 1980. "I was a poor college student working three jobs. So, I got a baby bib and embroidered it with a teddy bear. I said, this is a little gift for your new baby daughter."

I said, "This is really thoughtful. Our baby Tammy will love it." Tammy almost started crying hearing the name.

We did have two other 'T' names, Todd and Tracy, so we picked it to stay with the theme, but the 'other Tammy' as she identifies herself, was thrilled.

She went on to have a successful professional career, earning a Ph.D., teaching at several universities including Creighton and College of Saint Mary. She formed her own company, The Image Business, and is president and CEO. She is widely sought after for leadership seminars.

Jan Gradoville Schultz

Jan Gradoville Schultz was among many former students who baby-sat for us in the early 1980s. I called her Janet, everyone else Jan. One night she was coming over to baby sit, I asked daughter Tammy if she knew Jan's last name. Her response, 'Et' as in Jan-et. She still signs her texts, cards and emails with 'Miss Et.'

When she was a freshman, she told me that she was thinking about quitting school and moving back to Omaha where she had a boyfriend. I talked her into staying. It certainly changed her life.

I took her to her first job interview when she was a senior. One she turned down. However, the second worked and she became a reporter for the Imperial Republican. She said it would be a good start for a couple of years. Forty years later, Jan is still there. She married a local man and they raised three children there. Both have always been deeply involved in church and community activities.

When her oldest daughter was a senior, Jan brought her to Kearney for a college campus visit. They stayed with us. Sometime later, I called her only to find out her daughter wasn't coming to Kearney to college. She didn't want to follow in her mother's footsteps. She wanted to forge her own way, just as Jan had.

Bill Dunn

Bill Dunn talents as an artist, cartoonist and journalist endeared our friendship beginning when he was a student in the early 1970s.

At the time, I shared responsibilities as director of journalism and director of publications. One of my major publications was developing the recruiting brochure for the Admissions Office. I hired Bill to create the caricature-type artwork for one of those. When we were done, admissions director Wayne Samuelson could not have been happier. It was informative and cleverly presented with Bill's artwork.

That began our relationship. Bill graduated in 1973 with a double major in art and journalism. His varied career is testament to his ability in both fields. He started as advertising art and copy director at the Lincoln Journal Star. He was director of photography and graphics at Florida Today/USA Today, where he led the coverage of the Challenger disaster in 1986.

He was graphics editor of the Orange County Register in Santa Ana, California. There, he was a key player on news projects, including one that received a Pulitzer Prize. In 1990, Bill joined the Los Angeles Times as a graphics editor where he planned, organized and supervised the information graphics of the Gulf War which won the Judges Special Recognition Award and the Silver Award in the annual Society of News Design competition. Bill received a UNK Alumni Association Distinguished Alumni Award in 2008.

Don Briggs and Bill Dunn

After a stint at the Minneapolis Star Tribune, Bill returned to his home in Grand Island to become managing editor of the Grand Island Independent where he served until his early death at age 62 in 2014.

Among my most prized possessions is a caricature Bill did of me. It was a retirement gift from the Alumni Association. Bill has numerous other art pieces around the campus, particularly of the college antelope mascot. His 'Louie the Loper' was a staple of the Admissions Office and the athletic program for years.

Whenever I needed Bill's help, whether he was living in Iowa, Florida, California, Minnesota or back in Nebraska, he was always there.

Fred Arnold

Fred Arnold always appreciated the assistance he received to graduate in four years. At the beginning of his senior year, he solicited my help since, he said, "If I don't graduate, my dad will kill me."

Going through his career of nearly 40 years in the newspaper business, he reflected on those years in a letter to me.

Two things I remember, he said, "One was a journalism teacher saying his work was 'adequate at best' and you, who for some reason, always went out on a limb for me to get me graduated, interned and even found me my first job at the Shelton Clipper. It's been a wild ride since then.

"As Jimmy Buffett says, 'Some of it's magic, some of it's tragic, but I've had a good life all the way.'"

Fred bought his hometown newspaper, the Fairbury Journal-News in 1990 and had other newspaper and printing holdings.

He said he and his wife have sold off all their newspapers except one in Kansas and one commercial printing plant.

At any rate, he said, "I have been going through nearly 40 years of newspaper 'stuff' and almost 200 awards for journalism excellence that don't seem to mean much to anyone under the age of 40 anymore.

Jana Barnell Fitchett

Jana Fitchett has been family since her college days.

In her words, she said "JR was the one professor I counted on throughout college for advice and that camaraderie has continued throughout my lifetime. There's something special about his common sense and our mutual values that make our relationship special."

When Jana was a freshman student in one of my classes, she stopped me one day after class and said she had always been busy in high school and wanted to know how to get involved in college. She said she was considering the women's cross country team.

"JR advised me that I would be fine and would find a lot of activities soon. As always, he was right. By my sophomore year I had more activities than I could handle," she said.

According to Jana, one of her favorites was being president of Student Alumni Board, which I advised as alumni director.

"We had many great meetings (and parties) at the Alumni House," she said. "I remember one Halloween we all dressed up in the old clothes from the attic. As the student alumni president, I also was invited to the Southern California alumni chapter meeting. In addition to meeting great people, Jim took me to Disneyland for the first time."

Another favorite college experience was Gamma Phi Beta sorority where she held several different offices. She still travels with her five best friends from the sorority at least once or twice a year. "We've done it every year since college," she said.

Jana said, "JR's family became my college family. I was a regular babysitter throughout my college career and the best part (in addition to adoring the kids) was that they stayed out late so after the kids went to bed, I could invite boys over. I have hilarious memory of Jim and Lynn walking in to find basketball star Tim Higgins at their house."

Jana was a Coors campus rep, too.

Each year local distributor owner Wayne Gappa would select two seniors, one male and one female, to be his Coors reps. The brewery paid half of their salary, Wayne the other half. Mark Ryan was her male counterpart.

Wayne gave the reps $100 to spend every weekend and that was back when the bars had quarter draws. Jana said her job was to buy Coors for people at the bar. "To this day, I will never know if I had lots of friends or if it was just the free beer."

Her senior year, the Kearney distributorship won distributor of the year which was a huge honor.

Jana said to recognize the award, Bill Coors, Joe Coors and Jeff Coors flew to Kearney, along with the vice president of sales and the vice president of marketing for a huge party.

"Around midnight they asked me what I was going to do after graduation. Since I'd had about 50 beers, I told them I was going to work for them. The next week they flew me to Golden Colorado and got a job."

Following college, Jim kept me involved in the university by always inviting me back for events. That led to my serving as Alumni Association president in the 1990s.

Tracy, Lynn, Jana Barnell Fitchett, Tammy

"I've also kept in touch with the rest of the family. Lynn and the girls cut cake at my wedding and we danced to our favorite babysitting song 'Mickey.' Todd has always been our family photographer whether driving to Kansas City, Lincoln or Colorado. The photography memories are amazing.

"Tracy lived with us in the late 1990s before she found an apartment when she moved to Kansas City to work at the University of Missouri Kansas City. Tammy went to college at the University of Kansas so we got to have dinner with her every few weeks. Todd was dinner guest, too, while he was a photographer at the Kansas City Star."

Jana's background in marketing with Coors, Kraft Foods and GarageTek, Inc., led to a position on the staff at the University of Kansas beginning in 2006 where she is assistant director of the professional program. She teaches entrepreneurship and marketing. She has been recognized often for her outstanding teaching and leadership.

She has taught in the Israel Study Abroad program, mentored Ph.D. students, coordinated the university Morris New Venture Business Plan Competition and worked with KU student/athletes.

Peg Austin Bright

Peg Austin Bright earned a double major in math and journalism in 1974. Journalism became her career. Peg said she got interested in journalism by working on the yearbook staff her sophomore year. One of her sorority sisters urged her to get involved.

After graduating, Peg worked at the Kearney Hub and the University of Nebraska Omaha before studying in Egypt at the University of Cairo on a Rotary graduate fellowship. While in Egypt she met her future husband, John, an Australian working in the embassy.

When she came back to Nebraska after that year of study, she was required by Rotary to stay in the area to provide programs to Rotary clubs on the experience she had as an international student.

I talked her into teaching journalism and advising the student newspaper. Peg agreed but said she would do it for a year. My hope was for a longer time. She did stay from August 1977 until December 1980 when she resigned to join her husband in Egypt.

The way I learned about the marriage was when I had told her before she went back to Egypt the summer of 1980 that she needed to be back the middle of August for fall registration and staff meetings

When she was late, I wasn't happy which she said she could tell by my voice when she did arrive. "JR, she said, "we need to visit."

"We certainly do," I said.

Living nearby, she said, "I will come right over."

Typical Peg, she showed up with a big smile. What she told me was that she had gotten married that summer. She would teach first semester but was leaving to join her husband after that. What a huge loss for us. She was a great teacher and advisor to students.

John and Peg were married in Ajlun, Jordan. They have lived in Lebanon (during the civil war), Syria, Jordan and Burma. John resigned from diplomatic corps in 1989. They moved back to Canberra, Australia, where John practiced law until 2007.

When son Todd was an exchange student in Australia after they had moved back, we spent several days with the Bright fam-

Peg Austin Bright

ily. Since Peg still has family in Nebraska, she and her family are regular visitors to the Rundstrom home where we still manage to socialize with her friends in the Kearney area.

A story she did for me that was printed in the alumni magazine is a good example.

This is her story.

International travel can be a lot of fun – until you get mistaken for a Russian criminal. That's what happened to me last year (2014) when I crossed the Caspian Sea from Azerbaijan to Turkmenistan.

The experience wasn't as scary as you might imagine. I knew I wasn't Svetlana Sultandowna, and I figured it wouldn't be too long before the border officials figured that out.

I sat on the terrazzo floor while panicky immigration officers consulted by phone in the capital, Ashgabat. Within 90 minutes, digital comparisons of our photos confirmed that I wasn't Svetlana.

Soon after I cleared the border, I saw a Svetlana 'wanted' poster. She was smack in the middle of people-of-interest-to-Turkmenistan poster. I'll never know her special crime – it listed only a number – but I was pleased to see that she was 21 years younger than me.

Consequently, that wasn't my only weird border crossing.

My husband John and I have done a lot of international travel on the back of overland trucks. Dozens of times, we and our traveling companions have rolled up to a border expecting to be grilled, delayed, waved through or turned away.

Mauritania had 10 miles of the roughest no-man's-land terrain I've ever bounced along, and an amazing livestock market once we learned passport control.

Residents of a northern Nigerian village gave us a hero's welcome – with hordes of children cheering and running alongside the truck.

Relying on extremely bad French in the Congo, our driver Chris and I managed to beat down the price of fumigating our truck from $200 to $80.

Of course, our overland journeys have been about a lot more than border crossings.

Three years ago, we spent 11 months in Africa – traveling south down the west coast, then north up the east coast. There were 30-plus countries, 27,000 miles, millions of mosquitoes and 80 percent of our nights spent in a tent.

Floods of memories wash over me every time Africa is mentioned.

A three-day, 30-mile hike through Dogon country and a camel ride near Timbuktu, both in Mali. Skydiving in Namibia, canoeing in Botswana's Okavango Delta and gorilla watching in Uganda.

Then there was the day, the driver took a wrong turn in Awassa in southern Ethiopia, and we found ourselves in the middle of a parade to celebrate World Laughter Day. The media was so taken by our truck that we ended up on every broadcast in the country

We all took turns shopping for food, cooking, carting water and cleaning the inside of the truck. There were a lot of truck repairs, too. In the first two months, we had 13 flat tires. The radiator was a major problem from Ghana onwards and was the source of many delays, including a night in a remote logging camp in Gabon and five days in a village in northern Angola. Leaf springs broke in Kenya and again in Ethiopia, and were temporarily repaired with ratchet straps.

Nevertheless, we must have enjoyed ourselves because we signed up for another six-month adventure in the footsteps of that pesky Svetlana!

The second overland had 25 people from nine countries. It was a bit easier going than Africa, but offered plenty of memorable experiences.

We traveled much of the old Silk Road, including the ancient cities of Khiva, Bukhara and Samarkand. There were nights in yurts (a circular tent-like dwelling) in Kyrgyzstan, tents at 17,000 feet in the Himalayas and real beds in a cheap hotel in Tibet's capital of Lhasa.

We floated down the Mekong River, rode long distances in crowded buses and cramped ferries, ate enough noodles for a lifetime and explored dozens of temples.

I could start either trip again tomorrow, but I think I'll do something different instead. In fact, John and I are already booked on a four-month South American overland.

All of Peg's varied experiences are on her travel blog: leggypeggy.com.

Terry Zimmers

One August summer morning in 1972, Terry Zimmers walked into my office. Well, maybe she stomped in. She had driven 150 miles to take a two-week workshop called 'Supervising Student Publications.' She had recently signed a contract to teach English at Johnson-Brock High School. That included advising the school yearbook.

The only problem was when she went to register, she was told the class was closed. She would have to get the instructor's permission. His office was in Men's Hall.

At age 25, Terry was more than a little surprised to find the instructor wasn't much older than she was. She was prepared to plead her case – a new mother, a recent graduate and a promise to her superintendent that she would take the class.

I was reading the Omaha World-Herald when she came in. I had no idea why the class with 12 students would be closed. So, I called the Registrar to get her enrolled.

Terry continued to stay in touch She was an original member of two important groups on campus.

With admissions director Wayne Samuelson we developed the Alumni Admissions Advisers to assist the Admissions Office with recruiting. We identified alums across the state to contact prospective students, host events in their communities and share Kearney news. Each spring, we hosted a campus event with a weekend program and social. It was a great way to keep young alumni in touch with the campus. Plus, it was highly successful.

Terry also was a key member of the Alumni Association's women's mentoring program, Gold Torch Society as a mentor. An annual event provided speakers and ideas for both mentors and mentees. Terry also served on the Alumni Board and was Alumni Association president in 1991.

Terry wrote and printed on a dot matrix printer this humorous four-page pamphlet rendition with elementary artwork on each page.

Page 1: On a growing college campus a 'few' years ago, a shy but determined coed marched into 'Men's Hall' to demand her acceptance into a class which was classified 'closed' according to the Registrar. (picture of building)

On a growing college campus a "few" years ago, a shy but determined coed marched into "Men's Hall" to demand her acceptance into a class which was classified closed according to the registrar.

Page 2: After all, how would she feed her baby if she couldn't take the class that she promised her prospective employer she would take by the time school started up in August. (picture of young woman holding baby with house in background)

After all how would she feed her baby if she couldn't take the class that she promised her prospective employer she would take by the time school started in August.

Page 3: Luckily, when she approached the instructor of the class, who was casually reading a newspaper, the kindly 'old' gentleman took pity and let the beautiful 'young' coed into class. (picture of man behind desk with newspaper)

Luckily when she approached the instructor of the class, who was casually reading a newspaper, the kindly "old" gentleman took pity and let the beautiful "young" coed into class

Page 4: Thus began a wonderful friendship that has taken them as far as the Pacific Ocean and as near as the alumni house. Thanks for the past 20 years! (picture of ocean)

Thus began a wonderful friendship that has taken them as far as the Pacific Ocean and as near as the alumni house. Thanks for the past 20 years.

As Alumni president, Terry gave greetings to the graduating class at commencement. A school librarian in 1991, she used quotes from Dr. Seuss 'Oh, the Places You will Go' for her message. It was the last book Dr. Seuss would publish in his lifetime. Terry highlighted parts of it and I've always remembered it:

Congratulations
Today is your day
You're off to Great Places
You're off and away.
You have brains in your head
You have feet in your shoes
You can steer yourself
Any direction you choose.
It was a perfect message for the graduates.

Mike Burrows

Always the journalist, Mike Burrows had a way of expressing his appreciation for his college education.

"I have breaking news for you. Journalism graduates of the University of Nebraska at Kearney are as prepared to excel in the 'real world' as graduates of renowned journalism schools at major universities.

"How do I know that? I'm proof of it."

After graduating in 1979, Mike spent 40 years working in the journalism industry as a reporter and editor, including The Denver Post for the last 21 years of his career.

"Not once did I feel under-prepared for, or overwhelmed by, my job. And I thank KSC/UNK for that."

Mike said he felt his education was every bit as good as high-profile schools.

"And here is why," he said. "In journalism, nothing beats job experience and top-tier instruction. In Kearney, I was the beneficiary of both. The journalism faculty was as good as it gets."

Mike pointed out that before he graduated, he had accumulated plenty of job experience. He was the sports editor of The Antelope campus newspaper as well as a part-time sports writer at the Kearney Hub, where the terrific sports editor was fellow KSC alumnus Dan Vodvarka.

During my career, he said, this product of KSC and Columbus, Nebraska, MLB Denver Broncos of the NFL, the Colorado Rockies of MLB, the Denver Nuggets of NBA and Avalanche of the NHL.

He also covered events such as the Olympics, Final Four, World Series, MLB All-Star Game, Super Bowl, Fiesta Bowl, Rose Bowl, Orange Bowl, NBA Finals and Stanley Cup Finals.

My career was colorful, and it was based in UNK blue and gold.

39

Reunion

Reunion, n. All's Well That Ends W/Ellen

In 2015, the Sidney High School class of 1965 held its 50th reunion. As a former teacher and spouse of a classmate, I was invited. However, I was traveling out of the country, so had to pass on the invitation.

The reunion organizers then asked if I would write a 'congratulatory' note to the class for an introduction of a special booklet they were preparing. Naturally, I was most happy to do so.

This is that letter:

For all of us, it is amazing how quickly time passes. We graduate from high school, blink our eyes, and here we are 50 years later.

Now, on this special anniversary occasion, you gather to remember those formative years at Sidney High School and share the lives you have lived since then. I send my congratulations to the Class of 1965 as you laugh about many of the things that have occurred and shed some tears about other life-changing events.

Such is the nature of our travels.

In 1964, five years out of my own high school experience, I began my career in education at Sidney High School. It was a wonderful place where I spent three years teaching English, journalism and advising the Hi-Life newspaper and Trail yearbook. And, of course, it became an even greater part of my life after I met and married your classmate, Lynn Robinson.

Many of those memories are permanently embedded in my mind. Thanks in great part to the talents of Gary Boye and Diane Tobin, editors of the student publications, my job as advisor was simple. Give young, creative people a little direction and they will perform way beyond one's expectations. Such was the case with Gary, Diane and everyone else on the staff including John Bergner, Bruce Blanchard, Greg Fitzgerald, Diana Jamison, Bob Jay, Donna Landmesser, Rachel Perez and Cheryl Studnicka.

As a huge sports fan, I thoroughly enjoyed Maroon athletics, reveled in the wins and suffered through the losses. I have always remembered how the Trail staff struggled over the headline for basketball and finally came up with 'Success Should Come With Hard Work, But . . .' since the team had a disappointing win/loss record. But, like in life, there are successes and failures in every sport, football, wrestling, track, cross country and golf. The lessons learned in those and other activities like music, student government, student organizations and the things that happened outside the school, are certainly the fabric that every class member took through life.

When Lynn was a freshman in college, the year after graduating, she came home one weekend. Her sister, Leslie, whom I had in class, asked me if I would take her to a movie one night so she could go out with her friends. I said 'yes' and that 'yes' changed my life. After getting married in 1968, we had a great run in Kearney at Kearney State College and later the University of Nebraska at Kearney until her death in 2012.

Through the years we had the opportunity to return to Sidney often, stay in touch with her classmates and other Sidney High School friends. Those times, with family and friends, we all cherish. And we will continue to do so.

Remember the last page of your senior section of the Trail?

"It is an end, and yet at the same time, it is also a beginning. Beyond these halls lies the future, a future which they will be a part of, a future which they shall determine. They leave behind them noisy chats between classes, the slam of locker doors, well-worn pages of textbooks, invaluable friendships . . .and they go on and on. They go on to more distant horizons, higher goals, bigger dreams, a better life. They have a job to do. And they did it.

To reminisce about all of that is a very special time in your lives.

Enjoy your time together.

Jim Rundstrom

A couple of months after the reunion, I received the commemorative booklet that included biographical material from classmates along with a class picture.

In reading through the bios, one caught my eye, as did her picture.

Ellen Olsen Morledge

Address: Grand Island

Spouse or Significant Other: (blank)

Education: B.A. in Education – KSC, M.A in Education – Doane College

Employment History – 39 years in elementary grades 1 & 2; 32 at Jefferson in Grand Island, 7 at Northeast in Kearney.

Hobbies & Interests: Cooking, walking, traveling & golf. I like walking and exercising, but also relaxing on the patio with a good book and glass of wine. The man in my life the past three years is very attentive, has curly gray, black and white hair. Loves to take walks, a little shorter than me and knows that his place is at the bottom of my bed! I love Snickers – he's a Shih-Tzu!

She is also a dedicated mother of 2 children and grandmother of 5.

Ellen, Rita Jones, Karen Ensley, Betsy Jones, UNK
Distinguished Alumni Award winner Sandy Johnson

After reading that and a recap of the past 50 years, I emailed Ellen to see if she would like to have dinner sometime after I returned from a winter stay in Arizona.

As Ellen tells the story, she said 'yes' with reservations, wondering why a retired professor would be interested in having dinner with her. In my email, I asked what kind of books she read. She went to her good friend and neighbor to get a book reading update and her approval for dinner with a stranger.

One dinner led to another. She jokingly told me that I passed all of her requirements. I had hair. I was taller than her. I could afford to take her to dinner on a Friday night. These dinners led to social events with my friends in the Kearney area. The universal reaction of those friends after spending time with her was, 'She is special Jim. Don't screw this up.'

Which I have tried not to do ever since.

The ensuing years indeed have been special.

We have been on three Viking river cruises in Europe, traveled to Hawaii with my kids, to Alaska and the maritime provinces of Canada with friends, and to New England together as I completed my 50-state venture. We also spend some time in Arizona during the winter and enjoy myriad other activities.

With Ellen in the Netherlands

Ellen is also a terrific party planner. She has done it for her teacher friends in Grand Island through the years and now with our friends. We have had a luau, Halloween costume party, Christmas social, and Homecoming celebration to honor one of our friends, Sandy Holen

Johnson, who received a Distinguished Alumni Award from the Alumni Association and others.

As Ellen says, we are fortunate. We have good health. We have a home on a lake in Grand Island, a golf course home in Kearney, supportive families and tremendous friends.

A 'Collection of Friends' couldn't be more complete!

Enjoying times with friends

Row 1: Judy Wisdom, Kathy Horvath, Lori Klone, Susan Glascock, Jane Mattson, Rita Jones || Row 2: Tom Wisdom, John Horvath, Dave Klone, me, Doug Glascock, Kent Mattson, Lynn, and Roger Jones at a summer reunion

Watching the solar eclipse, August 21, 2017

Betty Jo Armagost, Ellen, Rita Jones, Galen
Hadley, Kathy Horvath, Marilyn Hadley, and Leanne
Elder are all dressed up for Halloween

John Horvath, Jim Armagost, me, Galen
Hadley, Roger Jones, Bruce Elder, Larry
Riessland in their costumes

Ellen, me, Marilyn Hadley, Galen Hadley, Roger
Jones, and Rita Jones enjoying the Sounds of Summer
music at the Museum of Nebraska Art

Steve Lydiatt, Jerry Dunlap, and Patty Lydiatt are
all smiles

Acknowledgements

My children: Tracy, Todd, and Tammy

Thank You!

Early in my leg recovery, Dale Butler suggested I write about my friends. He said, "You have great stories about so many of them." His encouragement was the start of this collection.

In the early 1980s, I wrestled with taking a new job and leaving Kearney. Lynn gave me the best advice I could have gotten after we had discussed the pluses and minuses of a career change which included a significant increase in salary. Lynn said, "Why would you want a different job? You are the happiest person I know. You can't wait to get to the campus every day. You love the students in Journalism, the alumni around the country, the wide variety of projects you work on. We have everything we could want or need. You are really lucky." She was right! These friends are a testament to that.

Todd, Tracy and Tammy played key roles in this several year process. I am not disciplined enough to work on a writing project, so this would not have happened without them.

Todd's photography skills added immensely. Tracy spent untold hours editing copy, providing ideas and publication directions. Tammy would always remind me of parts of stories I had forgotten.

When I found it easier to do something else, Ellen would provide the support I needed to get back on task.

Although they may not want to take any credit or responsibility for some of the things I have written, this has been a team project.

Cover Art

One of My most prized possessions is this caricature drawing by former student Bill Dunn. It was a retirement gift in 2008 and illustrates the impact of my association with the university.

CPSIA information can be obtained
at www.ICGtesting.com
Printed in the USA
LVHW051428221220
674884LV00015B/719